A French Soldier's War Diary
1914–1918

HENRI DESAGNEAUX

A
French Soldier's
War Diary

1914–1918

Edited by Jean Desagneaux
Translated by
GODFREY J. ADAMS

Pen & Sword
MILITARY

First published in France in 1971
This translation first published in Great Britain 1975
by the Elmfield Press
This edition published in 2014 by
PEN & SWORD MILITARY
an imprint of
Pen & Sword Books Limited
47 Church Street
Barnsley
S. Yorkshire S70 2AS

ISBN 978 1 47382 298 6

A CIP catalogue record for this book
is available from the British Library

Printed and bound in England
by CPI Group (UK) Ltd., Croydon, CR0 4YY

Pen & Sword Books Ltd incorporates the imprints of Pen & Sword
Archaeology, Atlas, Aviation, Battleground, Discovery,
Family History, History, Maritime, Military, Naval, Politics, Railways,
Select, Social History, Transport, True Crime, and Claymore Press,
Frontline Books, Leo Cooper, Praetorian Press, Remember When,
Seaforth Publishing and Wharncliffe.

For a complete list of Pen & Sword titles please contact:
PEN & SWORD BOOKS LIMITED
47 Church Street, Barnsley, South Yorkshire, S70 2AS, England.
E-mail: enquiries@pen-and-sword.co.uk
Website: www.pen-and-sword.co.uk

Contents

List of Plates

Introduction

It may appear unwise to publish a new work retelling the story of the First World War when almost everything seems to have been said about it and the event has become distant in our minds. However, Captain Desagneaux writes, 'one cannot imagine what the simple phrase of an official statement like, "We have recaptured a trench" really means'. It is precisely so that these words should no longer hide reality but show it in all its force, that this diary should be read. At the same time, the reader will discover that the First World War is not only that terrible holocaust with symbolic names like Verdun and the Chemin des Dames, etc., but a pattern of events which might seem comical, if they were not heartbreaking and too often tragic, due to the pettiness of military life, to the cowardice or blindness of certain leaders, to the bitterness which led to the mutinous revolts of 1917 throughout France. Like the 'Private', the reader sometimes desires to get back to the trenches and often ends up wondering what is the most 'deadly', the Front or the Rear?

Finally, fifty years after the event, these pages are the testimony of a man, of a race of men, who, because society and its moral principles, consciously or unconsciously, have changed, will scarcely be met with again.

It is not our intention to sit in judgement or to establish comparisons which are, after all, a matter of individual conscience. But it is obvious that a sense of patriotic duty pushed to such a degree of sacrifice, so much courage allied with so much modesty, so much honesty and uprightness even when confronted by stupidity and absurdity cannot but be remarkable. One can see in this diary as events proceed the birth of a new mentality which is not that of the author. This may appear justified, perhaps even necessary, but it certainly does not possess either its nobility or its grandeur. For two reasons, however, we do not desire to sing further the praises of a man whom you will discover in spite of his discretion and natural modesty: firstly, because this account, by its words and its silences, is a sufficient testimony for him; lastly, because I would not wish to be seen lacking in tact about a man who had so much himself, whom I deeply admire, who was my father. . . .

JEAN DESAGNEAUX

1914

1 August, *Saturday*

From the early hours, Paris is in turmoil, people still have a glimmer of hope, but nothing suggests that matters can now be settled peacefully. The banks are besieged; one has to queue for two or three hours before getting inside. At midday the doors are closed leaving outside large numbers of people who will have to leave on the following day.

In front of the 'Gare de L'Est', the conscripts throng the yard ready for departure. Emotion is at its peak; relations and friends accompany those being called up individually. The women are crying, the men too. They have to say good-bye without knowing whether they will ever return.

At last at 4.15 in the afternoon, the news spreads like wild-fire, posters are being put up with the order for mobilization on them! It's every man for himself, you scarcely have the time to shake a few hands before having to go home to make preparations for departure.

It's 5 o'clock, my mobilization order states: first day of mobilization—without delay. The first day is 2 August!

2 August, *Sunday*

Mobilized as a reserve lieutenant in the Railway Transport Service, I am posted to Gray. At 6 in the morning, after some painful good-byes, I go to Nogent-le-Perreux station. The train service is not yet organized. There are no more passenger or goods trains. The mobilization timetable is now operative but nobody at the station has any idea when a train is due.

Sad day, sad journey. At 7 a.m. a train comes, it arrives at its terminus—Troyes—at 2 p.m. I didn't bring anything to eat, the refreshment room has already sold out. The rush of troops is beginning and consuming everything in its path. Already you find yourself cut off from the world, the newspapers don't come here any more. But, on the other hand, how much news there is! Everyone has his bit of information to tell—and it's true! . . . A squadron of Uhlans has been made prisoner; the 20th Corps is already in Alsace. Everyone's talking about a 'Turpin Powder' the effects of which are supposed to be devastating.

At last in the afternoon I catch the first train which comes along: a magnificent row of first-class carriages (a Paris–Vienna de-luxe; all stock is mobilized) which is going no one knows precisely where, except that it is in the direction of the Front. The compartments and corridors are bursting at the seams with people from all classes of society. The atmosphere is friendly, enthusiastic, but the train is already clearly suffering from this influx from every stratum of society! The blinds are torn down, luggage-racks and mirrors broken, and the toilets emptied of their fittings; it's (typical) French destruction.

At midnight, I am at Vesoul; nothing to eat there either; no train for Gray. I go to sleep on a bench in the refreshment room.

The most fantastic rumours are going around; everyone is seeing spies unbolting railway track or trying to blow up bridges.

3 August, *Monday*

At 4.28 I leave Vesoul and arrive at last at Gray at 6.30 a.m. where I put myself at the disposal of the commander called Mennetrier. I am sent to Thaon station to see to the detraining of the troops.

The Eastern Railway Company is a source of admiration to everyone, but we are not used to such slow speeds. (The average for a military train is 2·5 kilometres an hour.)

Morale is excellent, everyone is extraordinarily quiet and calm. Along the track at level-crossings, in the towns, crowds singing 'La Marseillaise' gather to greet the troops.

The French women have set to it. They are handing out drinks, writing paper, and cigarettes. The general impression is the following: it's Kaiser Bill who wanted war, it had to happen, we shall never have such a fine opportunity again.

I don't stay long at Gray. At midday I catch the train again, am at Vesoul at 2.30, at Epinal at midnight. The area is already full of soldiers and there are no provisions to be found.

Rumour has it that German planes are bombing Luneville. Epinal is protected by the searchlights of its forts. The weather is heavy and stormy.

4 August

After three hours' stop, I leave Epinal at 2.59 a.m. and arrive at Thaon at 3.25. It's pouring with rain. Nothing to eat and no rest. The troops' billets have to be prepared immediately for they will soon be here.

No newspapers, no news.

The Epinal searchlights rake the sky incessantly.

6 August, *Thursday*

At 2 a.m. I get one hour's rest. The next train is due at 3. The traffic is intense, with the same enthusiasm and the same slogans 'Death to the Kaiser', 'String the Kaiser up', 'Death to the Boches'. The same caricatures: pigs' heads in pointed helmets. Bouquets, garlands, flags.

At daybreak two convoys of wounded—already!—are announced, one of 400 for Epinal, the other for Thaon. According to reports, an infantry battalion has been decimated by machine-gunfire.

The whole afternoon, trains arrive every two hours, artillery and infantry. When the troops get out the local children shower them with flowers.

Still no letters or newspapers, we know nothing about what is happening.

11 August, *Tuesday*

The troops continue to arrive. Three companies are in front of us. A battle somewhere between Nancy and Epinal, near Sarrebourg is expected shortly. There is cannon-fire at Blamont and Baccarat.

Casualties are starting to arrive and sunstroke is prevalent; people are not so enthusiastic now as in the first days.

The Territorials and Reservists are now arriving. They are not as orderly as the Regulars. Then there are convoys, lines of carriages of every description and limitless baggage.

The H.Q. of the 13th Company has been set up at Thaon. How many non-combatants, what a burden they are! They have requisitioned everything in the surrounding area, and the troops have to camp in the open.

Organization too is not what it should be. There is a train bringing a convoy of administrative personnel. It has been travelling for twenty-nine hours, and has no fixed destination. The men have no provisions and have not eaten for a whole day.

12 August, *Wednesday*

Decidedly there is not the same spirit as before. Perhaps it's due to the torrid heat, but the enthusiasm isn't there any more. The trains are not decorated with 'Death to the Kaiser' and the flowers have disappeared. Now it's slovenliness and orders bawled out as in manoeuvres. The leaders forget that it is wartime: the men get irritable when they see that the orders of the day prescribe polish, uniform regulations, and the pettiness of barrack life.

Disorder is rapidly replacing the order of the early days. The maimed and sick arrive from God knows where; only one train a day to evacuate them. The wounded, sometimes feverish, are forced to spend up to twenty hours at the station, in the open air without food or medical attention, left to themselves. Nothing has been planned for them by their companies, they just get rid of them and that's all.

The troops of Rambervillers and the surroundings come to fetch their supplies at Thaon! That is 30 kilometres there and another 30 back. The horses are worn out, and the units only get their supplies at 10 or 11 in the evening.

There is no more meat left to slaughter. The ranks can't get the order to requisition any as the Senior Supply Officer hasn't been seen for three days. Everyone blames everyone else. The locals don't want to hear anything about requisitions, they are tired of giving. The mayor (Lederlin) is willing to give up everything, provided that his factory is not touched, that he keeps his car, his horses, and can enjoy life as before!

15–18 August
Last arrivals: reserve artillery, transport columns, ambulances.

No news of operations, but people are speaking of some successes in the Vosges and in Belgium. Guns are firing away in the distance.

The latest trains are transporting vehicles of all sorts: buses, delivery vans from such shops as Bon Marché, Potin, Printemps. It's like a carnival procession.

At last, on the 18th at 1 in the morning, I am ordered back to Gray. The mobilization is over.

[At Gray, Desagneaux is ordered to take charge of the supplying of the 44th Division at Bruyères.]

25 August, *Tuesday*
Third night on my third-class bench. The guns roar incessantly. There is fighting at Rambervillers. It appears we have had a setback there

and abandoned the Saintes-Marie hill. The German heavy artillery is causing severe losses.

Otherwise, no news, the influx of troops just doesn't stop. The evacuation trains, too, arrive one after the other to carry the inhabitants of the towns and countryside towards the rear. The Germans are advancing and people are fleeing in front of the invader. They run but have no idea where they are going.

It's worse than the destruction of a town. Refugees arrive from all directions, a mixture of every class of society: the peasant carrying his little bundle; the worker with a few old clothes; small farmers, shopkeepers with their cases, finally the bourgeois, dragging along a dog or a trunk. Over Rambervillers, the guns thunder the whole day. One can see a sad procession of town and country folk, panic-stricken, fleeing in front of the enemy. Badonviller, Parux, completely destroyed, Blamont, Raon, Baccarat, Rambervillers. Men, women, children, and old folk are huddled together in any vehicles they could find. What a sad sight it is to see the old carts drawn by nags that even the requisition officers refused; these poor people, distressed, leaving their homes and their possessions, without knowing whether they will return.

There are families of seven, eight children walking along the road. An old man supported by a neighbour: he was a refugee in 1870 and is one again in 1914. A young mother pushing a pram in which her months-old baby is crying.

It brings tears to your eyes. All these people waiting, drawn towards the station—the railway is their only hope. They stand crowded together in the cattle-wagons, the youngsters don't understand, the others ask where they will be taken. It's an indescribable mess.

The guns thunder away, and convoys of wounded arrive to increase the confusion. Whole trains of them come, others leave empty to bring back 2,000 wounded announced at Rambervillers. Their limbs shot off, their heads a pulpy mess; all these bandages, spattered with blood mingle with the civilian population. The troops can only speak of the heavy artillery which shoots 10 kilometres and against which our 75s are powerless.

To make the pain even more unbearable, pessimistic rumours are circulating: the Germans are advancing, they will be here soon. The people push, shove, in their desire to leave.

A detachment of sappers is on duty at the station with 3,000 kilos of dynamite, ready to blow up the Bruyères tunnel in case of invasion.

Other rumours are going round: General Dubail has been relieved of his command. Our troops are said to have been massacred
at Sarrebourg. We are going through some alarming moments,
caught up in the fever which is gripping these poor people. The trains
are bringing thousands of human beings who crowd out the station
and the railway lines and make the civilian population ever more
eager to escape.

The station staff are working frantically, the guns fire non-stop.
The news is quite contradictory and night is going to fall without relieving the fear that the enemy could arrive at any moment.

2 September, *Wednesday*
I spend the night at the station waiting for orders that fail to come.

Convoys of wounded arrive in huge numbers; some German prisoners state that they don't know that England, Russia, and Japan
are at war with Germany. They don't know either that Belgium is
fighting to stop German troops passing through her territory. They
say, also that there is revolution in Berlin and they curse the Kaiser.

6 September, *Sunday*
A large number of soldiers wound themselves so that they can leave
the Front.

8 September, *Tuesday*
Throughout the area, at Dijon, Besançon, arrive panic-stricken
Parisians. They are fleeing just like those who lived near the frontier.

9–10 September
The news is better, the Germans are said to have been driven back
between Meaux and Verdun about 40 kilometres along a front of
200.

11–16 September
The weather is dreadful, troops board the train as the rain pours
down. All the soldiers who come back from the front speak about the
German heavy artillery. In the beginning, its effect was to start a rout
and the officers had to force the men back by threatening them with
their revolvers. Later on, the troops were quicker off the mark and the
Boches' shots were wasted.

25–26 September

We are embarking the Colonial Brigade of Infantry (Colonel Marchand) destined for Toul to resist a German attack made on Saint-Mihiel.

It's a real feat. These troops got their orders to embark at midnight, when they were fighting at Baccarat. After a 50-kilometre march, the first train-load is ready to leave the same evening.

Colonel Marchand informs us that he has a real epidemic of wounded hands, the men who are fed up with the trenches put their hands in the air to get a bullet and be evacuated.

He says too, that in his opinion the war will be long. He speaks of three years! All those who hear him think he is mad.

8 October, *Thursday*

At 4 a.m. I receive the order to leave at 5 to supply with provisions the 74th Division at Varangeville.

Here only a few shells have fallen, but the surrounding area has been the scene of hard fighting.

I take the chance of two hours off to go to Harancourt, 4·5 kilometres away where a large battle took place. Of the village (800–1,000 inhabitants), only ruins remain and scarcely seven or eight houses which are habitable. Round about, there are only half-destroyed trenches and graves. At every step, there is a cross, indicating a corpse, then shell-holes, followed by more. Huge fields which are the scene of desolation. There are piles of ruins everywhere, walls and roofs collapsed, and what has not been destroyed by cannon-fire, has been burnt. The burnt carcasses of horses are strewn here and there. Their church was even bombarded during a funeral service. One can see the outline of the catafalque and a shred of white cloth, the rest is merely ruins.

In spite of all this, the inhabitants return. One can see them prowling around what was once their home, searching through the rubble, crying over their fate.

I am back at Vezelise by 10 p.m., the guns are still firing.

20 December

I am handed a telegram announcing that I shall be relieved on the 23rd and should put myself at the disposal of Railway Control H.Q. What do they want of me?

F.S.W.D.–2

24 December, *Thursday*

I learn that I have been made assistant to the Senior Officer. An honour, perhaps, but what a change of life.

My life in the open air and journeys to adventure are over. Instead of work that demanded initiative I shall be in an office, amid my bosses from morning to evening with even my meals taken on the spot in the station refreshment room.

How lonely I feel! Won't my former friends have a jealous smile on their lips? What a sad end to my year. And tonight is Christmas, and my kiddies at home will put their shoes in front of the fire-place and I won't be there to see the joy on their faces tomorrow morning. I am alone, very alone and also quite sad.

1915

[From 25 December 1914 to 10 November 1915, Desagneaux is Assistant Railway Control Officer at Gray under Commandant Mennetrier.]

15 June

The cavalry divisions which had been massed at Arras, return to rest in the Vosges.

The Moroccan Division is returning too. I leave Gray on 4 July to carry out its disembarkation at Belfort. It was this division to which the attack at Arras was entrusted. They first attacked on 9 May, penetrated the German defence and routed them. But the order had been issued to advance only 800 metres. In one thrust, the troops advanced 5 kilometres; the reinforcements did not follow and the breach served no purpose. On a front 10 kilometres wide, the enemy artillery had been overrun and the Boches were in full flight. When the reinforcements did arrive, it was too late and the cavalry massed behind was of no effect.

The officers attribute this failure to General Foch who was ill-prepared; he thought it wouldn't happen and a breach was impossible.

The Moroccan Division, in the fighting of 9–10 May lost 9,000 out of their 15,000 men. It had with it the 33rd Corps, the 70th Division, and the 17th Corps, the latter not being involved in the attack.

A second attack on 16 June failed, as the enemy was ready this time.

The division is returning to Belfort to reform. Its infantry no longer exists and its artillery has been reduced by half. 300,000 shells were fired to prepare the attack and, as a result, the majority of the guns blew up towards the end of the fighting.

[From 10 November 1915 to 10 January 1916, Desagneaux is transferred to Besançon under Mennetrier who has now been made Lieutenant-Colonel.]

1916

10 January

Here is the date on which I am supposed to leave the Railway Control Service, but to go where, and to do what? No one can tell me. Lt.-Col. Mennetrier has not bothered about us one single day. If you are leaving, you don't count any more, he only had to ask the army. His motto must be 'Gold Braid, Brevity, and Selfishness'. In spite of numerous phone-calls, there are no orders for me. The army knows vaguely that we are expected. There are questions and deliberations, but we can't learn anything. The whole day will be like this—no orders. Even H.Q. has no idea.

I decide therefore to go to Remiremont to the Army H.Q. to find out what they want to do with me.

Training course for company commanders at Remiremont
15 January to 14 February

12 January

Here I am at Remiremont. I arrive at the Army H.Q. There, the same old story, they don't know what to do with us. They have heard that some railway officers were to join a unit, but that's all. No orders.

Then, once again, there are phone-calls to the Ministry and to central H.Q.—result—call again and we will see then. Finally, in the evening we learn we are to follow a training course for company commanders at Remiremont.

14 January

After settling in, I introduce myself with other friends in the same position to the Course Director, Lt.-Col. Petit. Great embarrassment. He has no orders to receive us and the course that we are supposed to follow is just finishing!

Still more phone-calls. Why are we arriving now? What is to be done with us? Must we join our regiment and return in five to six days for the next course?—Oh the beauty of French organization!

After long and frequent deliberations they decide to keep us for the end of this course and then we shall start the next one.

16 January

Sunday—Rest—The first time since 2 August 1914 that I see this word on a programme. I go climbing in the mountains with Jarrosson to get some fresh air.

17 January

First meeting of the course. There are about sixty officers. In lorries, we are driven to the Epinal Range for a session of trench destruction by tunnelling.

It's cold. The preparations are long. At the end of half an hour there is an explosion, then another, then a third. When night falls we leave.

18, 19, 20 January

Theory work on machine-guns. Tear gas, poisonous gases, etc., and finally manoeuvres to close the session.

The sessions are interesting, but how ordinary the officers are. The last offensive in Champagne, after so many others, cost us dearly in officers and all those who are here are former sergeant-majors or N.C.O.s. The companies are being commanded at the moment by sub-lieutenants.

21 January

Second day of manoeuvres in the mountains. We have no orders, we don't know anything—we march aimlessly.

25 January

Beginning of the new course.

On the following day, inspection by General de Villaret, commanding the 7th Army. An inspection of the battalion which is supposed to teach us something. It turns out to be a grotesque parade where this general is only interested in the men's bootlaces, the buttons on their greatcoats, and the hooks on their cartridge-pouches.

29 January

A Zeppelin flies over Paris and throws down bombs.

31 January
Exercises at Epinal and in crossing the Moselle.

1 February
Zeppelins over England. 54 killed, 67 wounded.

2 February
Practice with inflammable liquids, throwing bombs, torpedoes, and rockets at the port of Parmont.

4 February
Instruction on how to electrify barbed wire! What don't they invent these days to kill each other with!

5 February
Horse-riding lesson.
Practical work, some of it interesting some not, is succeeded by theory.
Practice at indirect machine-gunfire at Plombières.
It's cold, the snow is deep.

15 February
End of course, departure from Remiremont. The regiment is actually resting near Bruyères, where I shall go to join it.

Lorraine Sector
18 February to 29 May

16 February, *Wednesday*
Arrival at Bruyères at 8.50 a.m. Jarrosson and myself introduce ourselves to the staff of the 129th Infantry Division (General Garby). Great embarrassment. We are told that in the 2nd Infantry Regiments (359th and 297th) all ranks are filled. We are surplus to requirements and they don't know what to do with us. Yet again, orders have to be sought. While we wait, we have to go and join our Corps.
After lunch at H.Q., we go to Grandvillers (Vosges) where the regiment is billeted.
Lt.-Col. Mellier who is in command has no orders concerning us but welcomes us enthusiastically as his officers are of poor calibre.

I am immediately appointed company commander to the 22nd Company, 6th Battalion.

17 February

I take command of my company: three very ordinary sub-lieutenants (two butchers and a draper's assistant)—all Reservists—I feel the ill-will of the combatants against someone from the rear, but I'm the boss, and they don't dare say anything.

The men are aged between 20 and 42 years of age. A mixture which creates two cliques; the young ones team up with those of their own age, and the old 'uns stick together.

The N.C.O.s could be a lot better; they were corporals or even privates two months ago. They have no notion of leadership or responsibility. They are privates with stripes.

The regiment, which started fighting at the end of 1914, has fought successively in the Vosges (at Luige where it had a stiff time) in the north and finally in Champagne last October. It was part of the attacks of 5–6 October. Although the officers in the front line complained on several occasions that the barbed-wire fencing was not destroyed, the attack was ordered nevertheless (the order had been given, there was no going back, and the answer was always the same: it's not possible—our artillery has been firing for forty-eight hours, the wire is certainly cut).

It was under such conditions that the regiment attacked. In my battalion, two companies succeeded in getting through, the two others were stuck on the wire. These two were decimated or captured. The two others spent the day between the lines and suffered huge losses.

The same thing happened in the other battalions; the regiment lost about thirty officers. They were forced to promote whoever they could.

5 March, *Sunday*

Reconnaissance of the Arraye sector where we are due to relieve the outposts this evening. It seems that we are going to have to stay in this area.

For our reconnaissance we are driven by car to a hillock which overlooks the horizon, that's all.

It's 6 p.m., we leave Bouxieres, relieve the troops at Arraye at 8.30 p.m. It's my first relief. Fortunately the sector is quiet. The men take up their positions, my predecessor gives me my instructions and takes me on a trip round the sector. It's pitch dark; we stumble along the communication trenches at the risk of breaking our necks at every step. We don't see anything of note and come back.

6 March, *Monday*
My command post is in a cellar, under a group of flattened houses (the whole area is like this). The cellar is swarming with rats, and uncomfortable isn't the word.

In the morning, I go out and explore the sector; my company is guarding a front of 2 kilometres before the village. The Seille (a small stream) separates the lines.

The sector is quiet, some gunfire here and there: I make the most of it to visit the surrounding area. Everything is devastated, it's total ruin everywhere. One can see the fury that went into searching through the furniture and in destroying everything. The wardrobes are broken, the drawers torn out and scattered; everything of value has been taken, the rest is littered on the floor. Nothing is left except for some filthy scraps of paper and cloth and some broken odds and ends.

It's pitiful. In the presbytery, it's worse, if that's possible. They were even more bent on destruction there, seeing that it was the priest's home. The church is in an indescribable state of devastation.

8 March, *Wednesday*
At 4 a.m., grenades, machine-gunfire, a German patrol is sighted trying to cut our wire entanglements. Soon all goes quiet.

11 March, *Saturday*
Order to be relieved. We have been here for six days, and are beginning to get well organized in the sector and now have to hand over to others. That's the reason why our sectors are never organized.

Where are we going? We don't know. I am changing company. I have been given command of the 21st. It's the worst of the battalions; Its captain who has been made adjutant-major is a former regular N.C.O. and a real boozer. The sub-lieutenants who are there join in with their captain and spend their time drinking and gambling. Regretfully, I leave my 22nd Company which I was getting to know well.

The relief takes place at 8.30 p.m. without hindrance. We are going to be quartered at Bouxieres-aux-Chenes where we arrive at 2 in the morning.

12 March, *Sunday*

We settle in at Bouxieres. I take command of the 21st Company. As officers, I have four sub-lieutenants, a former Regular sergeant who is strong but simple; a wine-barrel of a butcher, a commercial traveller from Marseilles (formerly from the 15th Corps), and a steam-boat pilot who can't say one word without swearing.

At meal-times, two sergeants (why are they there?) come to join the group. The mess has a reputation for gambling and drunkenness. It's the only one in the battalion to which no one comes. My comrades pity me, while my superiors are counting on me to raise the morale of the troops. So, I start by sending the two sergeants to the N.C.O.s' mess. That will make two drunkards less with us.

13 March, *Monday*

I am terribly bored in this unsympathetic atmosphere where I have no friends. We are in a state of alert in a rotten little village of about twenty inhabitants. There's no escape. Even so near the front, with the prospect of leaving for it at any moment, it's barrack life. We clean the streets, in our quarters we make weapon-racks, polish everything, and do theory.

20 March, *Monday*

After hastily fortifying the front line, it is noticed there is no second line of defence in front of Nancy. Yet again, we work frantically. The guns are more active and it is difficult to go out. What to do besides? We are forbidden to ride, to leave the billet area, and to carry a camera. We would prefer to go to the trenches.

22 March, *Wednesday*

All the troops are working day and night: it's an orgy of digging, fixing wooden props, and barbed wire. Why didn't they do it earlier?

29 March, *Wednesday*

The sector is quiet, so the generals make the most of it to plague us with their visits.

30 March, *Thursday*

The artillery thunders. Armancourt receives 260 shells. An attack is expected, we are on the alert. If we were to attack, we would have to cover 1,500 metres of open ground, without a trench or anywhere to shelter.

1 April, *Saturday*

The day is beautiful, but troubled. There is firing all along the line. At 10 in the evening—it's hell, guns roar everywhere; to the right, to the left, in front, behind. Armancourt is ablaze. Its church is on fire, its steeple collapses. A splendid sight and a terrible one.

14–16 April

I am in charge of the wooden defence works at Lattes, Cugnes, and Rappont. These works were begun by the 121st Light Infantry Battalion, continued by the 120th and taken over by the 359th Infantry. I come to the following staggering conclusion: there is no over-all plan for these works, everyone building as he pleases. The 121st had their plan, the 120th didn't like it and modified what had been done, whilst the 359th has another conception of the defence works.

It's the third time that the work changes hands in three weeks!

Here is an example of such organization: the 121st was building machine-gun shelters at ground level; the 120th abandoned these to construct others beside them below ground.

The light infantry dug trenches 90 centimetres wide with a framework of interwoven branches built over them; in our regiment, the soldiers are digging them 1·2 metres wide with ready-built frames. We cannot therefore continue the work as it was. The shelters built by the light infantry are 4 to 5 metres square for a squad or half a platoon as necessary; in the 359th we want shelters of 10·2 metres by 4·5 metres for one platoon. So, after all the digging has been done and all the wooden frames are ready to be fixed, these are left to the rain, so that dimensions favoured by the 359th can be undertaken. When we leave, our successors will undoubtedly have their own method of work and that's how after twenty months of war, nothing is done. It's a waste of time and energy and a complete lack or organization along the line.

26 May

Yet again, there is talk of our being relieved and going to Verdun. They have been fighting over there for three months now, all divisions are going there in turn.

Verdun Sector
31 May to 5 July

10 June, *Saturday*
At one in the morning, order for departure at 4 a.m. We are to march in the direction of Verdun. That gives us an extra day of life! We are billeted at Rosières near Bar.

12 June, *Monday*
Issoncourt, last stage before Verdun. There is not much room as car-load upon car-load of supplies and munitions speed past us.

13 June, *Tuesday*
Reveille at 2 a.m. At 5, we travel by car and are put down at Nixéville, 6 kilometres from Verdun. We bivouac in a wood in a lake of mud. The guns fire angrily, it's pouring down. At 3 p.m. we are ordered to stand by to leave. We don't, however. We spend the night and the day of the 14th waiting, in torrential rain with mud up to our ankles. Our teeth chatter with cold, we are very uncomfortable. Although the troops have been stopping here for the last four months to go to and from Verdun, there is not one single hut or shelter. We camp in individual tents in thick mud. You should hear what the men say about it!

At 5 p.m., order for departure at 6.30. We are going to be quartered in the Citadel of Verdun. Faces are grave. The guns are thundering over there. It's a real furnace, everyone realizes that perhaps to-morrow death will come. Numerous rumours are circulating; we are going to 'Mort-Homme' which has been captured by the Boches; or to the Fort at Vaux. . . . What is certain, nothing good lies in store for us.

We arrive at the Citadel at 10 p.m. after a difficult march through the mud.

15 June, *Thursday*
We spend the day in the Citadel waiting. The guns fire ceaselessly. Huge shells (380s-420s) crash down on Verdun causing serious damage. I walk as far as the town; it's in ruins and deserted. One can't stay outside for long as shells are dropping everywhere.

The Citadel is a real underground town, with narrow-gauge

railway, dormitories, and rooms of every type; it's safe here, but very gloomy.

At 9 in the evening, we leave, not knowing our destination. We advance slowly through the night. At every moment huge shells come and explode on Verdun, at the crossroads, and in the direction of our gun-batteries which are stationed on all sides. We march in silence, everyone conscious of the seriousness of the moment.

At 1 a.m. we arrive at the Bras-Ravin Quarries, where we remain in reserve. No shelter, nothing, we are in the open fields at the mercy of the first shell.

16 June, *Friday*

Superb weather, but not far from us, it's a furnace of artillery fire. The Boches pump their shells at us, and our guns reply. What a racket! 150s and 210s scour the land on all sides and there is nothing anyone can do but wait. The battalion is massed in the ravine without any shelter, if their shelling was not at random it would be dreadful for us. The German observation balloons scan the horizon. Up in the sky, their planes search for us; we curl up in a hole when a shell bursts near us and it's like this until evening when orders arrive.

At 6 p.m. my company and another (the 24th) receive the order to advance with a view to reinforcing the 5th Battalion which is to attack on the following day. We leave, not knowing exactly where we are going; and no one has a map. We have a vague idea where the command posts are; guides are rare in this area where death stalks at every step. With difficulty, we move along crumbling trenches, cross a ridge to take up our position in the Ravin des Dames. The shells rain down, still no shelter.

We haven't eaten for twenty-four hours and don't know if supplies can arrive tonight.

17 June, *Saturday*

The attack is due at 9 a.m. The 106th is in charge with the 5th Battalion of the 359th as support. We have to recapture a trench at the top of the ravine that the Boches took from us the day before. We spend the night in the Bras-Ravin; hurriedly we dig a trench to give our men some shelter. Just beside us there is a cemetery where the dead are being brought at every moment. The guns fire furiously, from 3 o'clock it's hell. One cannot imagine what the simple phrase of an official statement like 'We have recaptured a trench' really means! The attack is prepared from 4 to 9 o'clock; all guns firing together. The Germans fire non-stop, ammunition dumps blow up, it's deadly. There are so many explosions around us that the air reeks of powder and earth; we can't see clearly any more. We wait anxiously without knowing whether we shall be alive an hour later.

At 9, the gunners' range lengthens. We can't see anything up in front any more. The planes fly low, signalling all the time.

At 11, after a relative pause, the cannonade starts up again. At 2 p.m. it's worse still, it's enough to drive you mad; the Boches are only firing their 210s and 150s, shrapnel explodes above us, we have no idea of what is happening or of the result. We are infested by huge black flies. You don't know where to put yourself.

At 6 p.m. I receive the order to reconnoitre the gun emplacements in the front line, as our battalion is relieving tonight. The shell-bursts are so continuously heavy that we cannot advance before nightfall and it is impossible to cross the ridge.

The wounded from this morning's attack are beginning to arrive, we learn what happened: our artillery fired too short and demolished our front line trench (evacuated for the attack), instead of firing on the Boches. When we attacked the Germans let us advance to 15 metres and then caught us in a hail of machine-gunfire. We succeeded in capturing several parts of the trench but couldn't hold them; at the moment out troops are scattered here and there in shell-craters. During the attack, the German planes bombed our men ceaselessly. Our losses are enormous: the 106th already has 350–400 men out of action, two captains killed and a large number of officers wounded. The 5th Battalion of the 359th, which was advancing in support was caught by gunfire and suffered heavily. The 19th Company hasn't got one officer left, in the 18th, three are missing. We have 32 Boches as prisoners. The positions are the same as before the attack—with our troops only being able to maintain the front-line position which they had previously evacuated.

At nightfall, the dead arrive on stretchers at the cemetery. In this, the Ravine of Death, they lay there, lined up, waiting to be put into the holes that are being hastily dug for them: Major Payen, his head red with blood; Major Cormouls, black with smoke, still others un-recognizable and often in pieces. A sad spectacle, which is repeated here every day.

18 June, *Sunday*

We have had to leave to occupy our new positions before our food arrived. It's the second day without food. We eat what little we've got amid huge black flies.

We are now stuck at the top of the ridge in a half-collapsed trench, without any shelter. The whole night there is terrible shelling; we lie flat and pray for any hole to shelter in. At every moment we are sprayed with clouds of earth and stone splinters. There must be an attack on the right, as one can hear the chatter of machine-guns! How many men are afraid! How many 'Croixes de Guerre' are weak at the knees!

The 210s make the ground quake, it's hellish, and explains the dazed looks of those who return from such a sector.

It's Sunday! Day breaks amid bursts of gunfire. We await orders. One can't think of washing or sleeping. No news: neither papers, nor letters. It's a void, we are no longer in a civilized world. One suffers, and says nothing; the night has been cold; lying on the damp earth one just shivers, not being able to breathe properly because of the smell.

The afternoon doesn't pass too badly. It's an artillery duel, where the infantry is not spared.

At 8 p.m. I receive the order to relieve in the front line a company of the 106th.

At 9 p.m. this order is countermanded, I am to relieve a company of the 5th Battalion of the 359th in the ravine, at the 'Boyau-Marie', near the 'Trois Cornes' wood where there are attacks every day. . . .

Orders and counter-orders follow each other; no-one has a map, or even a sketch. We don't know where the Boches are, but there is some fear that they will attack us on our right.

My company is all in a line in this trench which collapsed yesterday under the bombardment following our attack. A squad of machine-gunners of the 5th Battalion is buried in it; the following day at dawn we will discover all along the trench, corpses, then legs and arms protruding out of the ground.

Scarcely are we in position when the shelling restarts; the only shelter is small crannies in which one must curl up. We are being shelled from the front and from the flank. What fire! The ground trembles, the air is unbreathable; by midnight I have already eight wounded in my company.

19 June, *Monday*

We are expecting an attack at any moment. There is talk of recapturing the trenches with grenades. But what are our leaders doing? Ah, we don't see them here. We are left to ourselves, they won't come and bother us.

We try and make ourselves as comfortable as possible but the more we dig, the more bodies we find. We give up and go elsewhere, but we just leave one graveyard for another. At dawn we have to stop as the German planes are up above spying on us. They signal and the guns start up again, more furiously than before.

No sleep, no water, impossible to move out of one's hole, to even show your head above the trench. We are filthy dirty and have only cold tinned food to eat. We are not receiving supplies any more and have only been here for four days!

The afternoon and the evening are dreadful, it's an inferno of fire. The Germans are attacking our front line, we expect at any instant to be summoned to help. The machine-guns sputter; the ground trembles, the air is full of dust and smoke which scorch the throat. This lasts until 10 p.m. The fatigue party has to leave under a hail of fire to go and fetch our food just outside Verdun—6 kilometres there and 6 more back. The men go without saying a word!

20 June, *Tuesday*

The food supplies only arrive with great difficulty at 2 this morning. Still no water. When one has exhausted one's ration of coffee and wine, you have to go thirsty. By day, the heat is overpowering, we are surrounded by flies and corpses which give off a nauseating smell.

On the alert the whole night. Our position is critical. The Boches harass us. On our right the ravine cannot be occupied because of the shelling. The Thiaumont and Vaux works are being bombarded continuously. On the left, too, Bras and Mort-Homme are being shelled.

Yesterday my company had 2 men killed and 10 wounded.

The morning is calmer, but at 1 p.m. the firing starts up again. It's a battle of extermination—Man against the Cannon.

8 p.m. Night falls; time doesn't go fast enough—we would like it to be tomorrow already.

10 p.m. Great commotion, red and white flares, chatter of machine-guns, thunder of artillery. 400 metres from us, a new attack is unleashed upon our lines. Every man is at his post waiting, the whole night through. Will the Boches rush us from the top of the ridge?

Shells explode only metres from us and all around men fall wounded. We are blinded by the shells and by the earth they throw up, it's an inferno, one could write about such a day minute by minute.

Meanwhile, orders to stand by arrive. Ready we are, but those who are sending these orders, without knowing what is happening, would do better to come here to see the position we are in.

Today again, 1 killed and 9 wounded in my company.

21 June, *Wednesday*

Impossible to sleep, even an hour, the deluge of shells continues and the whole night frantic orders follow each other: you may be attacked, be ready! We have been ready for three days.

The night passes in an inferno of fire. Near Mort-Homme, calm has returned, the Boches are concentrating on Hill 321 and Vaux—it's hell out there—you wonder how anyone will come out alive. The shells, the shrapnel, the 210s fall like hail for twenty-four hours non-stop, only to start again; everything trembles, one's nerves as well as the ground. We feel at the end of our tether.

And what a responsibility! The chiefs tell us: keep watch, but no-one can give you any indication about the terrain; on our right, there's the ravine of Hill 321, but we don't even know the positions occupied by our troops and by the Boches. Our artillery itself, is firing without knowing our positions.

8 p.m. We have been bombarded by 210s for exactly twenty-four hours. The Germans have been attacking on our right since 6 p.m. My company at every moment receives the order to stand by to advance. It's a state of perpetual anguish, not a moment's respite.

We crouch there, with our packs on our backs, waiting, scanning the top of the ridge to see what is happening and this lasts until nightfall. We are haggard, dazed, hungry, and feverishly thirsty, but there is no water. In some companies there have been cases of madness. How much longer are we going to stay in this situation?

Night comes and the guns still fire; our trenches have collapsed, it's a tangle of equipment and guns left by the wounded, there's nothing human about it. Why don't they send the deputies, senators, and generals here?

9 p.m., 210s still, our nerves can't take much more. Can't move or sleep. There are no more shelters, one just clings to the wall of the trench. We wait. At 9.15 the bombardment starts again: the front line troops are so fatigued and jumpy that at every moment they

believe they are being attacked and ask for artillery support. Red
flares follow, our artillery does its best, it's hellish.

22 June

.At last in the evening I receive the order to relieve the 24th Company
in the front line. The whole afternoon there has been a deluge of
shells on the ravine, perhaps we will be calmer in the front line? But
where to go to relieve? A reconnaissance is impossible, no one has an
idea where the troops are exactly.

At 9 p.m. an avalanche of fire bursts on the ridge, the relief has to be
delayed, it would be impossible to pass. Is it an attack? There is gas as
well as shells, we can't breathe and are forced to put on our masks.

At 11 p.m. we leave. What a relief! Not knowing our front line
positions we advance haphazardly and over the top we find our men
crouching in shell holes.

My company is placed in one line, without any trench, in shell
craters.

It's a plateau, swept continuously by machine-gunfire and flares.
Every ten steps one has to fall flat on the ground so as not to be seen.
The terrain is littered with corpses! What an advance! It's dark, one
feels something soft beneath one's feet, it's a stomach. One falls down
flat and it's a corpse. It's awful; we start again with only one desire—
to get there.

My company occupies a broken line. Impossible to move around
in daylight. To the left, no communication with the neighbouring
company; just a hole 100 metres long; we don't know if the Boches
are there. In the centre, the same hole—occupied or not? I have a
squad which is completely isolated and stay with it.

The captain I am relieving (Symian) tries to show me the terrain.
He doesn't know it himself, dazed by four days spent up front amid
dead and wounded.

In a nightmare advance, we stumble forwards falling in shell-
craters, walking on corpses, flinging ourselves repeatedly to the
ground.

Ground where there lie forever men of the 106th, of the 359th,
still others of regiments who preceded us. It's a graveyard, a glimpse
of hell.

23 June, *Friday*

5 a.m. The bombardment starts up again fiercely. I get a shell splinter

in my lip. Nothing serious fortunately, as the wounded have to wait until evening to get their wounds dressed. One cannot leave the shell-hole even by crawling on one's stomach.

7 a.m. Alert. Commotion. The Boches attack. They are driven back by our return of fire. In the direction of Hill 321 huge attack which lasts three hours with wave upon wave of them.

The heat is oppressive. Around us the stench of the corpses is nauseating. We have to live, eat, and wait in it. Do or die! It's six days now since we had a moment's rest or sleep. The attacks follow each other. The Boches have succeeded in advancing towards Hill 321 and in occupying a part of the ravine behind us, where our reinforcements are.

The shelling has completely destroyed the trench where we were yesterday; the dead and the wounded are too numerous to count.

24 June, *Saturday*
Big German offensive on the right bank of the Meuse. This news arrived during the night. There is no question of our being relieved. Everything is silent and behind us, on Fleury ridge, the Boches continue infiltrating. We have been turned! There is no longer any doubt, as we can see enemy columns invading the terrain and their machine-guns are attacking us from behind while our artillery has had to move back.

Now something worse: my men, who have been suffering all sorts of hardships for the last seven days, are becoming demoralized. The word 'prisoner' is being whispered. For many this would seem salvation. We must fight against this notion, raise morale. But how? We can't move around, and only those near us can hear. They are all good chaps, devoted, who won't leave us and will form a bodyguard.

What are we waiting for? We don't know. Yet we can only wait for it: perhaps the attack which will kill us, or the bombardment to bury us, or exile even. We spend some anxious hours, without knowing how long this will last.

At 11 a.m. artillery is heard. Our batteries have taken up new positions and are opening fire, the Boches reply.

Impossible to eat, our nerves can't stand it. If we have a call of nature to satisfy, we have to do it in a tin or on a shovel and throw it over the top of our shell-hole. It's like this every day.

25 June, *Sunday*

Terrible day and night.

At 3 a.m., without warning, our own troops attack us from behind in order to recapture the terrain lost the day before on our right. These troops, without precise orders, without maps, without even knowing where our lines are, ventured off. They fell upon us, believing they had found the Boches. But the Boches were 100 metres in front, lying in wait and bursts of machine-gunfire cut them down in our trench. We thus have another heap of corpses and wounded crying out, but whom we are powerless to help. Trench!—well almost every evening we bury the dead on the spot and it's they who form the parapets!

At 6 a.m., the guns fire furiously and to add to our plight, our 75s fire at us. Terrible panic; six wounded at one go from a shell-burst, everyone wants to run for it. Agnel and I have to force these poor devils back by drawing our revolvers.

Major David is killed in turn by our 75s. Our green flares ask for the range to be lengthened, but with all the dust our artillery can't see a thing. We don't know where to put ourselves, we are powerless. Isolated from everything with no means of communication. There's blood everywhere; the wounded have sought refuge with us, thinking that we could help them; the blood flows, the heat is atrocious, the corpses stink, the flies buzz—it's enough to drive one mad. Two men of the 24th Company commit suicide.

At 2 p.m., our 75s start firing on us again. Our situation is critical. It is only improved when I send a loyal man at full speed with a report to the Colonel. Luckily he gets through.

26 June, *Monday*

Our 220 mortars bombard Thiaumont: we must recapture some terrain to give ourselves some room and to drive the enemy back in its advance on Fleury. We attack incessantly. It's four days since we have been in the front line and the relieving troops have been annihilated this morning during the attacks.

Rain replaces the sun; filthy mud. We can't sit down any more. We are covered in slime and yet we have to lie flat. I haven't washed for ten days, my beard is growing. I am unrecognizable, frighteningly dirty.

27 June, *Tuesday*

The guns thunder the whole night: the men who left to fetch the food at 10 last night haven't come back. Still longer without food or drink.

4.30 a.m., first attack on Thiaumont and Hill 321.

9 a.m., second attack. All around us, men are falling: there are some only 5 metres from us in shell-holes, yet we can't help them. If you show your head, you get a burst of machine-gun bullets.

The whole day, incessant firing: the Boches counter-attack; we drive them back by our rifle fire and with grenades.

My company is rapidly diminishing, we are about sixty left now, with this small number we still have to hold our position. In the evening, when the men go to fetch supplies we are really at the mercy of an attack. Still no relief.

28 June, *Wednesday*

Hardest day to endure. The Boches begin to pound our positions, we take cover; some try to flee, we have to get our revolvers out again and stand in their way. It's hard, our nerves are frayed and it's difficult to make them see reason.

At midday, while we are trying to eat a bit of chocolate, Agnel's orderly has his back broken beside us; the poor chap is groaning, there is nothing we can do except to wait for nightfall, and then, take him to the first-aid post, and will we be able to? The wounded are so numerous and we have so few men left that those who can't walk sometimes have to wait for forty-eight hours before being taken away. The stretcher-bearers are frightened and don't like coming to us. Furthermore, the nights are so short, that they can only make one trip. One trip: four men to take one wounded on a stretcher!

1 p.m., it's an inferno: the Boches undoubtedly are preparing to attack us. Shells scream down on every side: a new panic to be checked. At 6 p.m. when we are dazed and numb, the firing range lengthens and suddenly everyone is on his feet, shouting, the Boches are coming. They attack in massed formation, in columns of eight!

These troops who, moments ago were in despair, are at their posts in a twinkling; we hold our grenades until the Boches are at 15 metres, then let them have it. Guns bark, and a machine-gun which survived the avalanche of shells is wreaking havoc.

The Boches are cut down; amid the smoke, we see dozens of dead and wounded, and the rest retreating back to their trenches. Our commanding officer, thinking that we are hard-pressed, sends us welcome reinforcements. They will be useful for supplies and taking the wounded away.

Only around 9 p.m. is it quieter. We help the wounded who are waiting to be taken away. Our shell-holes are lakes of mud. It is raining and we don't know where to put ourselves: our rifles don't work any more, and we can only rely upon our grenades which are in short supply.

This evening, still no relief; another twenty-four hours to get through. It gets colder at night, we lie down in the mud and wait.

29 June, *Thursday*
Our fourteenth day in this sector. The bombardment continues, our nerves make us tremble, we can't eat any more, we are exhausted.

Yet still no relief.

30 June, *Friday*
Attacks and counter-attacks. Frightful day—the shelling and the fatigue are becoming harder to bear. At 10 a.m., French attack on Thiaumont; the artillery fires 12,000 rounds of 255s, 550 of 220s, and the 75s fire at will.

The din began at 6 this morning; the Boches reply furiously. It's hell, we are getting hit more and more often, as our position is the favourite enemy target. The majority of the shells fall on or around us. The shelling will last ten hours! And during this time we expect an attack at any moment. To make it worse, my own company is hard hit. A 210 falls directly on a group of men sheltering in a hole: 3 killed and 2 seriously wounded who drag themselves up to me to plead for help. A minute later, a second shell sends a machine-gun flying, killing 2 more men and wounding a third. It's panic stations— the men run, and under a hail of gunfire, I have to force them back again with a revolver in my hand. Everyone goes back to his post, we set up another machine-gun and keep watch.

At 10 a.m. and 2 p.m. first and second French attacks on Thiau- mont. The Boches harass us with their fire. Our heads are buzzing, we have had enough. Myself, Agnel, and my orderly are squashed in a hole, protecting ourselves from splinters with our packs. Numb and dazed, without saying a word, and with our hearts pounding, we await the shell that will destroy us. The wounded are increasing in numbers around us. These poor devils not knowing where to go come to us, believing that they will be helped. What can we do? There are clouds of smoke, the air is unbreathable. There's death everywhere. At our feet, the wounded groan in a pool of blood; two of them, more seriously hit are breathing their last. One, a machine-gunner, has been blinded, with one eye hanging out of its socket and the other torn out: in addition he has lost a leg. The second has no face, an arm blown off, and a horrible wound in the stomach. Moaning and suffering atrociously one begs me, 'Lieutenant, don't let me die, Lieutenant, I'm suffering, help me.' The other, perhaps more gravely wounded and nearer to death, implores me to kill him with these words, 'Lieutenant, if you don't want to, give me your revolver!' Frightful, terrible moments, while the cannons harry us and we are splattered with mud and earth by the shells. For hours, these groans and supplications continue until, at 6 p.m., they die before our eyes without anyone being able to help them.

At this moment, the hurricane of fire ceases, we prepare to receive an attack, but fortunately nothing happens.

We look at one another, our eyes haggard, trembling all over, half-crazy. Is it going to start all over again?

At last, at 8 p.m., an order: we are to be relieved. What a cry of joy from those of us left. We wait anxiously and it's 2 a.m. before the replacements arrive. Our information is quickly passed on. Soon it will be dawn and we have to cross the zone before sunrise. Tiredness disappears, and our limbs regain enough strength to escape from these plains where at every step the guns have done their work; corpses of men, carcasses of horses, overturned vehicles, it's a horrific graveyard all the way to Verdun. We halt, the guns are rumbling in the distance, we can breathe at last; we call the roll, how many are missing when their names are called!

Our time at Verdun has been awful. Our faces have nothing human about them. For sixteen days we have neither washed nor slept. Life has been spent amongst dead and dying, hardships of every sort and incessant anguish. Our cheeks are hollow, beards long and our clothes thick with mud. And, above all, we have a vision of these horrific days, the memory of a comrade fallen in action; each one of us thinks of those who have not returned. Despite our joy at being alive, our eyes reveal the crazy horror of it all.

During the struggle, whole regiments have melted away. The 129th Division doesn't exist any more. The 359th has lost 33 officers and 1,100 men. My company, with the 22nd, had the heaviest pressure to bear. Both resisted all the German attacks. They prevented their descent into the ravine and therefore the complete encirclement of the area.

1 July, *Saturday*
After being relieved, we are quartered at Bois-la-Ville, in the same camp where we stopped on the way here. We arrive at 2 p.m., exhausted. We fall into bed and sleep like brutes.

2 July, *Sunday*
At 8 a.m., we pile into cars, glad to leave this ill-fated region far behind. We get out at Ligny-en-Barrois at 2 p.m. We spend the evening at ablutions.

5 July, *Wednesday*
Promoted captain.

Bois-le-Prêtre Sector
14 July to 1 October

14 July
On leave from the 6th to the 12th, I rejoin the regiment at Liverdun. At 1 a.m. we depart for Villiers en Haye. Leave is over; our division, now reformed, is to take over a sector at Bois-le-Prêtre.

The battalions are reduced to three companies, the fourth forming the Infantry Corps.

25 July, *Monday*
Trench life begins anew. It's calm for the moment, but things will soon hot up. This sector was guarded for eighteen months by the same troops; Reservists, they had got into bad habits, and not intending to kill themselves, they even went as far as fraternizing with the Boches. They passed cigarettes to each other in the trenches. They even sang songs together. Our division has orders to stop all this and to harass the Boches. Our gunners don't have to be asked twice and pound the enemy who are not long in replying. Attacks follow and the sector will become harder.

1 August
Two years of war!

The weather is glorious. Life is spent in the trenches, in shelters crawling with rats and lice. We can hardly see it's so gloomy.

The sector is hotting up, two officers (Lymian and Poli) of the 24th Company are seriously wounded.

5 August
Heavy mortar fire; for the second time, my shelter (a fragile cellar) collapses. These mortar-shells are causing huge damage, but the rats, bugs and fleas are even more formidable. The Medical Corps don't even bother about them. We live in filthy squalor.

At 1 a.m. we relieve the front line in the 'Marseilles' sector near Regnéville. The sector is bad. Every day the trenches are devastated by mortar-fire. My command post is 10 metres below ground, with water streaming in from all sides: every morning we have to bale out 10–15 buckets-full of water coming from a near-by cesspit. How damp and dark it is! Our candles are continuously snuffed out by the gusts of air caused by the mortar shells. When outside, one is at the mercy of these or grenades.

23 August
In the evening, huge din. Flares are sent up all along the line. A barrage starts up and lasts until 2 a.m. The cause of it all—a German patrol and the panic of the 23rd Company on my right, which lost a man taken prisoner.

2 September
Relief due at 4 a.m. The mortar-fire is still intense: there are many dead in the 22nd and 23rd Companies who are in the lines. At 3 a.m. there's a dreadful din which recalls Verdun. Firing on all sides. My company is alerted, we are ready to march. Relative calm at 4.30 and the relief takes place at 5. We are going to be billeted at Griscourt.

[Captain Desagneaux spends 2 October to 20 November in man-oeuvres at the Bois l'Eveque camp. He is then posted to the Somme.]

Sector of the Somme
20 November 1916 to 14 January 1917
22 November
At 4 a.m., we arrive at Beleuse (Somme). The men are exhausted and, after twenty-eight months of war, we still find the same problems.

Our billets are not ready and there is no straw. The locals refuse their rooms because they are not paid. And what billets! They are mud-walled sheds, which are half-falling down and draughty. The men grumble and rightly so, the buildings are pigsties rather than habitable dwellings. The artillery was here before us and there's horse dung everywhere—it's disgusting.

I am lodged in a miserable alcove without any heating. With a simple iron bedstead and mattress, neither sheets nor blankets! I manage to get myself a sleeping bag, I am freezing cold.

Food is not cheap in the area; eggs are 35 centimes, ham 10 francs a kilo, bread 2 francs. It's a miserable existence and tomorrow perhaps, the men will be asked to go and get themselves killed.

28 November
We go through Hericourt, Flocourt, which are completely destroyed. The sector seems organized and compares favourably with Verdun. There are communication trenches and shelters. It is said that we have nine successive lines of artillery and that we are supposed to attack Mount Saint-Quentin with the 20th Corps, then Biaches, La Maisonnette, and Barleux, reserved for the 12th. The preparation would last eight days and the attack would take place on 10 December, but what don't they say?

To hear the troops who are in the sector, the mud is frightful. Everyday, there are large numbers of men suffering from frostbitten feet.

20 December
I leave at 4 a.m. to reconnoitre the sector. My company is in front of Barleux, no reserve at the Bois de Boulogne Quarries.

At 11 p.m. the relief takes place. The sector is troubled. There is shelling with gas the whole day. One could be at Verdun.

There are masses of planes in the sky, through a gap in the clouds I count 45 French ones. Two of them fall in flames on our lines.

In the distance, about 30 balloons observe. Is it the preparation for an attack? The shells rain down and the men are overcome by the gas. On the right, the Moroccan Division attacks unsuccessfully.

22 December
Rain and mud. Many men evacuated with frostbite. Hard day. A lot

of gas. Heavy bombardment of our Quarry. The shelters are insufficient and several collapse. Munition dumps explode all around us. It's enough to drive one mad.

The orders for the attack are handed to us: an attack along a front of 18 kilometres, with five days of artillery preparation and twenty-four hours of gas. Sounds promising. The artillery of the 6th Corps is to put a smoke-screen over Mount Saint-Quentin. Everything is prepared down to the last detail, our first objective is Barleux, then the Somme.

23 December

The order to attack is countermanded. Why? It's a secret. Political reasons they say. Questions in the House on our effective strength and munitions. Also affairs in Greece and Rumania.

Our situation is the same, heavy shelling, gas, etc. . . . I go to link up with the Moroccan Division on our right. There, the sector is awful. The Arabs like attacking, but work, never. As a result, the communication trenches fill up more and more every day. You can't use them unless you want to sink in mud up to your waist. If you are unlucky enough to fall into a shell-crater, the mud comes up over your head. There are men in the front line who are buried up to their waists. Some officers tell me that during their last relief, they had to pull men out of this morass by means of ropes.

29 December

At 9 p.m. relief, and what a relief it is! The guns thunder. It is raining and the communication trenches are no more than a cess-pool, we advance at 2 kilometres an hour and we have 11 to do before reaching camp at Cappy. The night is black as ink and it's difficult to find one's way. Finally we come out of the trench near Flocourt. It's the most dangerous cross-roads as gun batteries are installed not far away and the whole zone is shelled. The road is like a quagmire. We get tangled in telephone wires, stumble into holes, the mud coming up to our knees, sometimes up to the thighs. We mark time in some places rather than advancing, with only the shell bursts to show us the way. It's a nightmare; some men fall in the holes and are sucked down, we are obliged to help them. Artillery shells explode all around us, but we can't take cover as the mud is too thick. The shells follow us as far as Herbécourt, with mud splashing up on all sides, it's mad.

30 December

The men returning from the trenches are hideous; they are covered from head to toe with a thick coat of sticky mud. Their equipment, rifles, and packs form one huge ball of it. One has only to see this to realize what our troops are suffering. The cry is unanimous here: let Poincaré, let Joffre, the deputies, journalists, and senators come and live here a bit with us. The war will end quicker.

1917

11 January

No-one will miss this sector where—if we didn't carry out the attack intended—we suffered severely from the mud and the cold. In the battalion, we have about 10 men wounded and more than 80 with frostbitten feet.

Where are we going? Some say to Woere for a night attack in the Oise. It's the unknown, always the unknown. Tonight, at last, I have a bed and I get undressed for the first time in a month.

Vosges Sector
15 January to 14 May

16 January

After a very cold night, we arrive at 11.30 at Corcieux. Forty-two hours travelling. Our legs are numb. We are going to the Vosges region. At last, no more mud, no more plains stretching as far as the eye can see, just mountains. It's freezing hard, 40 centimetres of snow on the ground, superb! And no more cannon-fire.

We are billeted at Grange. Already rumours are circulating: we are supposed to be going to the trenches in four days. The cook heard it from the postman who got it from the Colonel's cyclist, who heard it from the cooks or the orderly or the secretary, etc. It's the same old story. But in this sad existence without ever knowing what tomorrow will bring, one hangs on every word.

28 January

Orders for hand-to-hand combat during which we are supposed to capture prisoners. It's true that the General is at Saint-Dié, the Colonel at Raon (18 kilometres from the lines), the commander himself at Pierre-Percée, what are they risking?

10 February

Note from the Colonel: 'There are too many men in the rear; keep an eye on your fatigue parties; avoid too many men leaving the trenches. The front line must be attractive and not repulsive!!!' Why, therefore, don't we ever see him in the lines?

15 February

How to launch an attack! The General commanding the Army says: In four days, I need at least three prisoners. The Chief of Staff decides: Division X in $3\frac{1}{2}$ days you will capture a prisoner; Division Y ditto, Division Z ditto.

The General commanding these divisions says to his colonels: In three days you will bring me at least one prisoner.

The Colonel decides therefore: Attack in forty-eight hours on such a position. That's it.

The whole plan is elaborated, of course, kilometres in the rear on a map. Is it possible?—they don't think about that. They need prisoners. When they get down to details and it's a question of placing their mortar-fire—like La Chapelotte—they realize it isn't.

But it is too late. The order has been given and there's no going back as the officers don't want any disgrace. That's how our attacks are always unfruitful and only result in losses and sometimes prisoners taken from our side. How much simpler it would be to study first what is possible and where, then give orders after these details have been settled, rather than say: I need that, there, in such a time!

24 February

An attack was made yesterday by the 10th Battalion, 30 minutes artillery fire as preparation. Result: nothing, except 7 killed, including Captain Govignan and 15 wounded, some seriously.

After the preparation, the company leaves its trench; one minute after, the Boches unleash a terrible barrage of fire and the troops are cut down during their retreat. Govignan is killed in his trench.

On the other hand, on Hill 607 (Fave Valley) the Boches try a surprise attack, after having sneaked up on our men, and capture 20 prisoners.

3 April

Still cold, windy and wet with snow on the ground. We are relieved at 11.30 p.m. Quartered at Raon-L'Etape at 4 p.m.

4 April
Many men get drunk. Morale is low. They are fed up with the war. Certain corps court-martial some men for desertion, theft, insolence, etc.; after condemnation (with reprieve in the majority of cases) they are transferred to another corps. My company is infested with them. Special strictly disciplined companies are needed, prison sentences are useless.

1 May
Yet again, we leave the sector for the unknown. General Nivelle is relieved of his command. Pétain now becomes General Chief of Staff for the Army.

Meaux (Maintenance of Order)
31 May to 16 June

1 June
The spirit of the troops is turning sour. There is talk of mutiny and of troops refusing to go to the lines. The 'bad hats' amongst them are more vociferous.

3 June
All the companies are in a state of turmoil; the men are receiving letters from friends informing them of the present spirit and urging them not to march; the ringleaders are becoming insolent; others are trying to influence their comrades. My company does not escape this plague: a squad, under the sway of its corporal, refuses to fall in, the men claiming that they are ill. Just as we move to take them to the guardroom, they run off in the fields and insult the N.C.O.s. Some only return the following day.

I have five court-martialled, to get rid of the worst. Alas! that's just what many want—a motive to be court-martialled, so as to spend a year in prison; they are counting on some future amnesty and, during their stay in prison, they will be far from the Front. Once again, it will be the good who will go and get themselves killed and the scoundrels who will be protected.

In addition, a law has just increased the men's pay: first payment today. These men who are getting 20–30 francs rush to spend them on drink; drunkenness all along the line. Command becomes difficult.

5 June

I sit in judgement at the court-martial. What a procession of rogues! How stupid they seem in front of their judges. In their company they tried to be smart, insulted their superiors, tried to get their chums to desert; here they are now, sheepish, not daring to look up, full of repentance.

At 7 p.m. General Garbit and General Méric come and ask for me at my quarters, to entrust me with a confidential mission.

The Army is becoming more and more a prey to this ill-feeling; those on leave on their return home from the front, are assailed by agitators who, going as far as uncoupling the trains, urge them not to return. I must go to Meaux to re-establish order.

7 June

On my arrival at Meaux at 9.30 I organize my troops at the station and in town.

One platoon for the town and hospital (where there's a load of brutes), two platoons at the station, one in reserve, in case of need.

At 3 p.m. the first train of those on leave arrives at the station from the front. As soon as the train enters, you would say a horde of savages, all the doors opening on both sides and the men flooding out on the platforms.

Shouts, insults, threats fly in all directions: death to the shirkers at home, murderers and pigs that they are; long live the Revolution, down with war, it's peace we want, etc. We empty the station to avoid conflict; the station staff don't dare show themselves. That's why I'm here. At La Ferté-sous-Jouarre a company of machine-gunners is on guard. At Chateau-Thierry, a company of light infantry: each division has its zone.

4 p.m., second train. The troops invade a garden. The owner kindly offers to let them pick flowers, provided that they don't do any damage. There is one mad rush and everything is destroyed; they attack the house too, the windows are broken and the blinds torn down. They shout the same cries and insults: Death, long live the Revolution, down with war.

5 p.m., third train. As soon as it stops, the troops surge out menacingly. There is an empty train in the station: the men seize stones and break every window. During the journey, a man had fallen on the track and had had his foot cut off. The military superintendent of the station—a lieutenant aged 55—rushes up with four men and a

stretcher to carry him away. Seeing his white band the troops call him a murderer and beat him black and blue. It all happened so quickly that the attack passed unnoticed and we found this officer lying unconscious on the platform after the departure of the train.

Often scenes such as these happen at the last moment, as the train is leaving, so that we can't intervene.

The trains are in a lamentable state; the doors are wrenched off and thrown on the track during the journey; all the windows are broken, and the seats slashed to ribbons.

That's the state of affairs. My men are well-disciplined and will be ready to act at the first signal. I have no fears in this respect. The situation however, is delicate, for how can I intervene, should the need arise, with 30 or 40 men, against a frenzied horde of a thousand individuals, the majority of them in a state of intoxication?

8 June

At La Ferté, same scenes. At Chateau-Thierry a deputy station-master is injured. A general who was on the platform was manhandled and had his képi snatched from his head. The guard intervened and a man was arrested. Immediately all the troops got off and uncoupled the train. They only consented to leave when their comrade had been freed. The station staff are so ill-treated that they go into hiding when these trains arrive and refuse to do their duties.

At Meaux my guard duty passes normally. My men, well turned-out, parade in the town and are a source of admiration to everyone. This is because at Meaux, there are only fatigue sections: bakers, drivers who have no idea of smart turn-out, good discipline.

The day passes with the usual cries of: down with war, death to the slackers, long live the Revolution and that's all, except for a drunk who got out a razor to show how he cut the Boches' heads off; we cart him off to prison.

12 June

The postal service informs me that letters seized are full of threats and plans for revolution. No-one hides the fact things are bad and everyone is fed up.

15 June

We are ordered to stand by to leave; the 327th Regiment is replacing us. The 359th engaged in the Chemin des Dames has changed armies and we must rejoin it.

17 June

The 'good days' at Meaux are over and as we return to the lines the shirkers back there with their cars (Crème Simon, Fromages Gervais, Maison Potin, Nerveux de Paris, and many more) continue their gay life. These gentlemen have got their own restaurant there where no outsiders are allowed and every Saturday the ladies of Paris come and join them. Concert, dancing, it's a real orgy. This is what the men have seen and that's why this evening they grumble.

Sector of the Chemin des Dames (La Royère)
17 June to 10 July

17 June

Before the relief, sinister news reaches us. During the day Captain Pelletier is killed, as well as Ruby and his three officers who are either killed or seriously wounded in their shelter.

At 9 p.m. we leave Chassemy to relieve a company in reserve at Filain—what a relief! Despite the fact that this evening it's terribly hot, we have to cross two bridges where the 210s crash down and Rouge-Maison farm where batteries are installed and where the deluge of shells is even thicker. We cross the bridges without a hitch, but at the farm it's a real barrage of fire. Obliged to make a detour, one section gets lost and can only rejoin us at dawn. We arrive at 2.30 a.m., thirsty and exhausted and not a drop of water.

During the relief, I have 1 man killed and 5 wounded.

18 June

Superb weather. From 4 a.m., the German planes are above us, two of them flying as low as 50 metres to machine-gun the trenches. It's an awful sensation to hear this tac-tac-tac and the whistling of the bullets. We curl up and anxiously wait until the engine gets fainter. We watch the plane fly casually away—ours aren't there and he can do as he wishes.

Every day there are repeated attacks on our lines: the Germans are gradually recapturing the ground they lost. The Chemin des Dames is virtually theirs. We have relieved here the 3rd Artillery Company because they refused to march any more and the Boches took advantages of this ill-feeling to recapture the terrain.

Throughout the region, there is talk of nothing but mutinies, of troops refusing to relieve their comrades. Near Braisne, they have massed Moroccan and Algerian troops whose role will be to force the troops to go to the trenches if the need arises. It often happens that troops in the lines spend three or four days longer there because their replacements refuse to march. It's the spirit of the day.

In the evening, after a day of overpowering heat, I leave at 10 p.m. to reconnoitre the sector which we must relieve tomorrow. I go with Agnel and Veyren. We have to cross bridges which are fired on incessantly by guns. Near the lines, no more trenches, everything is destroyed; the companies can no longer repair the damage done each day, one advances the best one can over mounds of fallen earth. Flares soar above us continuously and bursts of machine-gunfire keep us pinned down; we can't see anything—that's what they call a reconnaissance! At last, from the light of a shell-burst, not far ahead, we discover dozens of frightened faces sheltering in every available cranny of a shell-hole. We get our breath and then obtain some rather vague information; the Boches attack every day, they don't know exactly where their lines are and after a brief glance on a sketch-map, our comrade says: 'Go quickly and see you tomorrow.'

We leave hastily: he was right, the shells arrive in their hundreds exploding everywhere, the men can't work any more, the communication trenches are virtually non-existent—they are blocked and one moves around with great difficulty. The fatigue parties for food and munitions get lost in the maze. At every moment, they are obliged to take cover. It's frightful. Then there's the procession of wounded that they carry from the lines to the rear; we can't find a way back and decide to cross the plain. But soon we are lost, there are communication trenches in all directions, barbed wire entanglements to go round, we don't know where we are any more, I am covered in perspiration and we have to wait for dawn to get our bearings again. Sad, sad life. How is it one doesn't die amid all this?

19 June

In the evening at 10 p.m. we relieve the Couteau trench at La Royère.

20 June

The day is spent at the mercy of an indescribable barrage of fire, we expect an attack at any second, everyone is at his post. There's no thought of eating, we are dreadfully thirsty, but we haven't a drop of water to drink, we must wait until nightfall when the fatigue parties will bring some water-bottles.

21 June

I am at last granted some leave. It's very welcome and I don't wait until evening to depart with my orderly, we dash off. Once again, we have to cross the Filain ravine, and go past Rouge-Maison farm under heavy artillery fire; we take cover, run 100 metres only to take cover again, finally arriving at Wailly. Here, it's desolation, ruins everywhere. We get our breath back in order to cross the bridges at full speed; shrapnel explodes continuously, we are far away now and can breathe again. We are soaked with sweat, but I am going on leave, danger doesn't matter.

I reach our combat H.Q., hidden in a wood, no shelter or tent. It's beginning to rain; in the open air, I get undressed, open my case. I change and wash and at 9 p.m. I make my way to the station. Still 6 kilometres to go. 18 kilometres of lines! How can any civilian imagine what it means to leave them behind?

I spent my leave at Pornichet. On my return expected to find the regiment resting. It is always in the front line.

6 July

My battalion has been on duty in this sector for twenty-five days. We are supposed to be relieved by the 10th Battalion which is returning to the lines.

At 1 a.m.—no-one. We learn that the troops don't want to come back. Then, about 3 a.m., when day is about to break, small groups of four to five arrive. They have no idea of who is there or where to go; finally at almost 4 a.m., when the recalcitrants have been brought to reason, the relief takes place, but in what conditions.

It is light. The German planes fly over us and signal our movements. Then it's a deluge of shells of all calibres. The trenches are destroyed— we have to cross open spaces in full view; we run, bent double pursued by bursts of machine-gunfire. Miraculously, we reach our position without too much harm.

The departure of the 10th Battalion for this relief was a real epic. The battalion was quartered in a mushroom farm with the divisional H.Q. At the order to put their packs on, nobody moves, the candles go out, it's pitch black. Every time an officer lights a candle, it is immediately put out. The parade cannot take place. To the orders given them, the men reply with sneers and insults. The officers of the division try and intervene, but they are manhandled. Time passes; some men pick up their packs and see reason; their comrades disarm them. The officers, fed up with their lack of success, draw their revolvers and threaten. Immediately a loading of rifles is heard on all sides. The officers parley with the men, trying to inspire some to set a good example, and thus encourage others to go. Failure. Some officers equip with their own hands their loyal soldiers and make them leave one by one. This decides others. And that's how, first of all, we saw small groups arriving.

All this took place before the eyes of the division, the regiment's honour is tarnished. It will be utterly lost on 8 July.

8 July

Memorable day for the regiment. In Champagne (1915) it lost 22 officers. At Verdun, 23. This evening there will be at least 32 officers and 2 battalions (the 5th and the 10th) with their commander and their adjutants, almost completely lost to the enemy. It was obvious that the Boches would venture an attack on our front: the levelling of the trenches pointed to it as well as the fact that the enemy now had a view of our positions after completing its recent daily series of conquests. The violent bombardment of the past forty-eight hours had slowed down; the night seemed to calm.

At 3 a.m. suddenly a terrible cannonade rips through the air; everything is a mass of fire in the front and the rear of the regiment, it's a deluge of fire. I go outside with Agnel and Blanchin. We get ready, for we feel that we will be called upon to march. But how will we succeed in crossing the barrage of fire to reach the front lines?

At 3.10 a.m. the telephone is cut, nothing works any more, only couriers.

At 4.15 I receive a note from the Colonel telling me to alert my company and the squad of machine-gunners which is with me and to stand by. This note left the Colonel's command post up front at 3.15. What happened since? The cannons roar. We are extremely anxious.

At 4.55 a second note ordering me to come immediately with all my men. At the same time a soldier rushes up like a madman shouting that he had escaped from the hands of the Boches, that the whole line is taken, that the 5th and 10th Battalions are prisoners.

We will therefore be expected to counter-attack. I assemble my company; nobody jibs, not a murmur.

Blanchin leads up front. I stay behind to encourage the hesitant.

At 5.50 a.m. we are all on our way. In a long line we cross communication trenches, then we have to pass by the Gerlaux farm where a barrage of 210s creates panic and finally the ravine where the Colonel is stuck amid an inferno of fire. How we advance, how we get through, how we are not blown to smithereens at every step, nobody knows. We stumble on; explosions everywhere, we fall flat, get up again, it's raining, we are swimming in mud, but we go forward in a hurry to escape this furnace, to get there at last only to find perhaps worse still.

It's impossible to get through this zone unharmed. At every step the trenches have caved in, we have to advance in the open, we go onwards nevertheless, streaming with water, covered in sweat and mud, panting, and with a lump in our throats. They are counting on us and we press on and on. Some wounded are lost en route. We arrive at the Colonel's ravine. I put my company at his disposal.

We have no idea of the situation, except that the few who escaped say that the Germans are in possession of our lines, that the two battalions—5th and 10th—don't exist any more, their commanders Poli and Grillot, their adjutants, Caldeiron and Pipat, all the officers— with the exception of Sevey who escaped—are prisoners. The front is wide open, the Colonel has nothing in front of him, his papers are burnt, he is preparing to leave.

When I arrive, everyone heaves a sigh of relief. A single squad was guarding the ground occupied by two battalions. Immediately three platoons of my company go into action. The shells fall like hail, we are repeatedly knocked to the ground, it's a miracle even to advance. The other two companies of the 6th Battalion (Morel and Vivet) have been sent for; they will arrive two hours later.

One of my platoons supplies fresh munitions and rockets. We left without any food; besides, no one is hungry, the situation is too critical. Three German prisoners are brought in. Some of ours who managed to escape begin to arrive and we learn what happened.

The attack was instantaneous and very violent with special troops. It was made easier by the fact that our companies had evacuated the front line to allow our artillery to destroy the enemy trenches. The Boches pressed on and arrived at the second and then the third lines where they caught everyone by surprise. The machine-guns didn't fire a bullet as the gunners were all sheltering below ground because of the heavy gunfire.

Time passes; the guns roar, it's awful. I receive the order to organize a line joining what is left of our front line on the right with our third line, our last defence. We have to infiltrate, fighting with grenades. The Boches are everywhere.

In my command I have my three platoons, two of the 38th Company, one of the 22nd, one of the 23rd and a few escapers who have returned to fight. The important thing is to hold our ground; the men are hard pressed and covered in mud. We hold nevertheless. Orders come thick and fast, and gradually, we drive back the enemy advance parties and retake some of the lost ground.

The hours seem never-ending, the gunfire relentless, everything trembles. The dead and wounded are numerous.

At 4 p.m. we learn that the relief will take place this evening: the 159th has been alerted and is arriving in motorized transport. The 344th in reserve at Braisne and the 68th Infantry Division refuse to march.

Night falls, heavy barrage of fire on both sides. Behind us, in the Colonel's ravine, it's a deluge of 210s. I am ordered to lead a counterattack to recapture the Scutari trench occupied by enemy troops. Their machine-guns decimate one of my platoons; artillery fire pins us to the ground. On three occasions we launch an attack; in vain, the men can't take any more.

At last, the relief arrives, they don't know exactly where the lines are or where the enemy is. It's total confusion. By now the Germans have organized their mortars which are firing in batteries of six, pounding our positions. In one single platoon, I have 7 killed in a twinkling.

We leave in this gunfire. Once again we have to cross Ostel, Rochefort farm, Wailly, all heavily bombarded. There's not a square metre without several shell holes: corpses everywhere, ruin, devastation.

We go out of firing range and breathe at last. I am tired out. We have been in a state of alert for days now and no one has eaten for thirty hours. At the first opportunity I sink into a deep sleep. However, we still haven't arrived, we have to leave again, it's only at 9 a.m. that we reach Chassemy.

Right up to the end of the campaign, the 359th will bear the brunt of responsibility for this day. Those in command will resent the fact it allowed itself to lose two battalions. However, those left, who fought, who prevented the enemy from advancing, are they responsible for this? And those who are captured, who wilted under the attack, are they as responsible as all that?

Fate played its part in this affair. Our commanders knew that an attack was imminent: to try and stop it, an artillery barrage had been decided for 8 July at 3 a.m. on the enemy lines. This barrage was intended to disorganize the enemy troops. Because of it, all our soldiers had been withdrawn from the front line, with the exception of some look-outs. All our men (by order) had piled into shelters, of which there were few, with the result that captains couldn't act.

At 3 a.m., at the same time as our guns were opening up, the enemy unleashed its attack. Nobody realized, and the enemy, meeting no resistance in its advance, arrived at the shelters which were packed with troops. A few grenades thrown here and there filled our men with panic and whole groups were captured.

This is how the day started. The Germans, however, didn't advance any further and by the end of the day a large part of the ground lost was recaptured.

It was, however, a fatal day for the regiment, all citations were refused to those who had done their duty. Is not war made of capture and of losses of men and terrain on both sides?

Yes, but the chiefs had noticed the ill-will the 10th Battalion had shown in going to the line a few days previously. This was only one step away from accusing these same troops of having surrendered— and this step was soon taken.

Vauxhaillon Sector
10 July to 1 November

10 July

At 6 a.m. motorized transport takes us to our new quarters at Puiseux.

What are they going to do with us? The regiment no longer exists; it is necessary to reform it: only the 6th Battalion has 450 men, the others are reduced to nothing. We have no illusions; if we stay in the area, it's to be back in the lines in a fortnight.

11 July

While waiting we sleep and wash; fleas abound. The men need fresh underwear to be really clean; but as if by chance, there is a shortage of it! The men grumble and indeed it's pitiful to see these men who have not washed for a month, obliged to keep on wearing the same smelly rags, due to the fault of some supply officer who doesn't know what the front is like or to some commander lacking in foresight. Oh, how they ought to make all those in the rear come and see what it's like in the trenches!

12 July
Rest!—Not likely. It's back to paperwork, the trials and tribulations of barrack life start all over again. Report to be written on the effective strength of my company, report on losses, report on cart-ridges, on flares, on body-linen, report on those sick, report on tools, report on a drunk, on noise heard the night before in a billet, report on everything.

Now the shells are far away, the chiefs reclaim their rights, and already visits and inspections are announced. Then, as if these were new, I get a note on the cleanliness of the billets, on the measures to be taken in case of fire, a note to put a hand-rail on the attic ladders, note on weapon-racks, on the cleaning of equipment, on the visiting of the sick, etc., each note, of course, means another report to be written. We are already wishing we were back in the lines.

14 July
Fun and games for the men; but their heart really isn't in them; there are too many recent absences in the ranks.

Our departure is announced for tomorrow. On the programme four or five marches.

15 July
Assembly of all officers of the division. General Pétain wants to address us. Everyone is there, from the general to the youngest sub-lieutenant.

Painful meeting which does nothing to raise morale. Pétain enters, cold, stern, 'How many deserters in the division?' he asks im-mediately. We look at each other. We were expecting something else. And, after asking the amount of losses, declaring that we should not count on reinforcements to bridge the gaps, he finishes with these words, 'You must re-discipline this undisciplined division. Gentle-men, that's all I have to say to you, good-bye.' And he leaves slam-ming the door of his car.

Brute, is that the way to raise morale and to ask people to go and get themselves killed?

A cloud hangs over us, we are sickened. It's definite, then; the battalions surrendered—they were undisciplined—at least in the minds of these gentlemen. And those of us left, who did their duty, who are still ready to do it to the very end, must they expiate the fault of those who had one moment's discouragement or cowardice?

Pétain has not shown himself a great leader, at the very least not human. There were so many ways to make us feel what he wanted— without saying it!

Who was he talking to?—to Reserve officers in the great majority, who all held their ground. At the beginning of the war, they said scathing things about us, we were considered as duffers, and yet, what would they have done, what would they do without us? We who are alone at the front whilst the Regular soldiers—who had chosen war as their profession—are in the rear, in depots or sheltered in H.Q.s or other services.

Pétain has said that after three years of war the men are tired. Yes, and with these ways of treating them, they will end up destroying the goodwill of those men—Reserve officers—who left their homes full of courage and who receive no reward for it. All the 'Croixes de Guerre' are for the Regulars, nothing for us.

We return dismayed: an hour later, first note to say that it's urgent to take a firm hold on all units, and to put discipline into action. How many fine words?

17 July

Departure from Bournel en Vallois at 4.30, quartered at Béthisy-Saint-Pierre.

During our marches we have the generals, the Colonel on our back. The men are overloaded with equipment, often wearing worn-out shoes that can't be replaced. They plod along. But they are exhorted to step out firmly, rifles erect, to keep in line, with head up. Perspiration rolls off them, but they must button up their overcoats, put their helmets well over the forehead, guides in their places and ranks-closers in the rear, those blankets are not properly rolled, that haversack isn't in its place, that tool is on the right instead of the left . . . it doesn't stop and, on all sides, the men murmur: 'You don't say that when we are in the lines; we never see you there. Come and line us up when we are leaving for an attack.'

Then after the troops, it's the vehicles' turn. Too heavily loaded— doesn't conform to the regulations—a favourite word in wartime.

In spite of it all, our fine bunch of lads, aged between 35 and 40, march, march, to the bitter end.

18 July

In the column a soldier has no overcoat. Why? asks the Colonel in his gruff voice. 'Colonel,' replies the man, 'captured on the 8th, I managed to escape from the hands of the Boches, but my overcoat stayed with them.' 'If it was to return in that state of dress, you would have done better to stay there too,' replies the Colonel. That's it, raise morale! But is this the way and is it hardly surprising that there are anti-militarists?

We are all sickened. The notes pile up: forbidden to do this and that. Then, 'Those who leave their weapons behind in the trenches are cowards, we will take their Croixes de Guerre from them.'

And of course the captain is held responsible for everything. Sad, sad life! When will we see the end? When? The Russians are retreating again, there's lassitude everywhere! The same words are on every lip, 'I am fed up!'

24 July

Every day exercises are brightened up by a visit from the Colonel. Nothing but criticism. Everything is bad. Never any encouragement, all we do is daft. How he makes us hate the army, and yet again, the men murmur, 'Just come to the trenches, we never see your bl—dy face there.'

Why criticize all the time? Let them teach us if what we do is wrong. We are all Reservists here, we don't come from Saint-Cyr. But to show us what? We know what trench life is like, but does he? In that case criticism is safer than advice. Raise morale!

3 August

The fourth year of war is beginning. We leave Coeuvres at 4 a.m. It rains without stopping the whole day. We are going to be billeted at Taincourt (north-west of Soissons). We are in recaptured territory: there is nothing left, all the houses have been burnt, the trees cut down. It's destruction in all its horror. We are installed in a cellar full of mud, without a door. It's frightful—and we have to live in it.

4 August

Some local inhabitants are returning to their villages—to see what is left; they are full of sadness and of memories of relations shot on the spot in 1914. The government is supposed to be building huts to lodge the inhabitants, but these poor people, who have lost everything, will only be able to live in them if they can afford the rent!

15 August

Yet another fine sector! Pointed, exposed on two sides with a small command post in a trench which communicates with the Boches, the sentries of both sides only 15 metres apart. It's a continual grenade battle. Two platoons in the lines, one as support, and the other in reserve. Only the latter has some form of shelter at Moisy farm which is itself no more than a heap of stones. The other platoons must live in the trench and dig for themselves under the parapet benches or seats where they can rest. It's impossible, of course, to light a fire; at night when the food arrives we have to eat it cold.

The first day ends badly. At 9 p.m. whilst Agnel and I were having barbed wire installed in front of the command post, the Boches take fright. Suddenly, a shower of grenades fall upon us, we are surrounded by fire and smoke. Flares soar in all directions, the Boches think they are being attacked and unleash a barrage of mortar fire. With great difficulty we get back to the trench, everyone is on the alert. Already those in the rear are worried. What is happening? For an hour the hail of shells covers us with earth, and the trenches cave in. All around us, cries and moans from the wounded. In a flash I have 3 killed and 8 wounded, in one platoon alone. Then towards 11 p.m., calm returns, I can rejoin my post after ensuring everyone is in his place. There will be work to do tonight.

Midnight—there's a procession of wounded to my post; we are walking in blood. The first-aid post is beside me. There are men with legs and arms blown off; one of my best soldiers has an eye hanging out and a leg shot off: he is at his last gasp and begs me to kill him. We have to tie him on his stretcher. They carry him off, but he dies on the way.

Sad, sad life.

4 September

A note received at 6 a.m. orders me to go and follow a ccurse for company commanders at Montigny-Lengrain.

At 7.30 I leave with my orderly. We go through Vauxhaillon, Antioche, La Tuerie Courson, Leuilly. I arrive only at 7 p.m.

What a dump! and of course nothing has been prepared. It's complete and utter negligence. We are 40 officers, but there are lodgings for only 10 of us—those who arrived first. The others are herded into the town hall and sleep on straw. I miss my company already.

7 September

The course begins. It is terribly boring. The captain in charge is disconcerted at having to teach other captains. He thought he was only getting sub-lieutenants.

He merely states that we know as much as he does and he has no idea what to say to us.

14 September

Visit to see tanks at Champlien. They are big ones from Saint-Chamond which are not very mobile and don't much inspire confidence. But how many officers there are in this service! You can't see anything but commanders, lieutenant-colonels, and colonels.

18 September

Visit to a fighter squadron near Missy-aux-Bois. There are 45 Nieuports here but not one is available. Suffering from a defect, they cost pilots' lives during trials and have to be rebuilt. The fact that we are way behind in aviation is not hidden from us.

25 September

End of course. What have we learnt? Nothing.

26–27 September

I rejoin my company in the second line at Antioche farm. It is forty-five days now since the regiment has been in the lines. There's no question of departure, rather we must think of the next attack. It's our punishment for 8 July which they never let us forget. The men, covered with fleas, grumble.

6 October

We continue to prepare the attack, despite the fact the companies are skeleton-like; I have fifty men less, certain platoons have no leader, or N.C.O.s. The other companies are the same; they could scarcely put fifteen men in the lines per platoon, with one machine-gunner instead of three. But what does this matter; the division must attack; nothing must be said.

10 October
A note this morning from the general of the division ends thus: 'You are in mud and water; you are tired, I know. . . .' Is it wise, therefore to leave in the lines men tired of sixty days of sector and to prepare them for an attack? If one abuses the men like this, can there be little wonder that they are let down?

The men are not easily hoodwinked. They do not understand, for example—us too—why, although there is a rota laid down for duty in the sector, do the same ones all stay behind, without ever coming to relieve their comrades in the front?

14 October
I am invited to lunch by General de Corn. An affable man but one who prefers liaising with those in the rear rather than with the Colonel's companies in the lines. It's so much easier too to travel by car on a road!

We naturally speak of the forthcoming attack: Oh! it will be a piece of cake, the Boches will be routed . . . there's no question of our being relieved now or even later.

18 October
At 1 a.m., I receive the order to have the Elfes trench reconnoitred and to bring back some prisoners. Agnel advances with his platoon at 5.30. He is met with a formidable barrage of fire and this and the German grenades and barbed wire stop him getting through. We'll have to try again, I have 4 men wounded.

Shortly afterwards, an officer in charge of mortars comes to check with me the ranging of his guns. With amazement, I learn that the spot where we are supposed to attack has not yet been shelled. He is proceeding by trenches and will only fire on the Elfes trench in forty-eight hours! Thus as usual, orders have been given in the rear, from a map, without knowing what was happening up front. Afterwards they wonder why our attacks are not successful. Result: the men, who had left in high spirits, are now discouraged, and don't want to attack any more.

19 October
The attack is postponed for twenty-four hours.

21 October

Heavy shelling, life is becoming unbearable. The Boche is standing his ground. Here is the report that I send on our situation: 'Every day the lines are completely flattened, the shelters are shaken to the point of collapsing. In spite of the courage of my men, I need all my energy to make them stay in such a dangerous spot. In certain places there are no trenches of any sort, just a field full of holes which we arrange as best we are able. There is little liaison possible between ourselves. We can't rest and defence is all the more difficult as our weapons, filled with earth, are not working properly; flares are also in short supply.'

'Fatigue is also making itself felt, it is becoming dangerous therefore to leave in the lines troops after seventy days of sector. We are at the mercy of an enemy attack.'

And what I don't mention is the filthy state we are in, covered in mud, we can neither wash nor sleep, piled as we are, thirty of us into a hole big enough for ten.

22 October

Gas the whole night—masks on all the time. We are supposed to attack today—but no news. There are rumours that preparation on our right is insufficient, that things are not going too well, that at Laffaux, the Boches have captured our front line, etc. . . .

We know nothing, how long are we going to stay here? The barrage of fire is getting heavier and heavier, our shelters cave in and the lines are a shapeless chaos of slime in which we have to find some cover. Two of my liaison officers are wounded at my side.

23 October

Notes the whole night. 'D' day has arrived, 5.15 a.m. is the hour. Our guns open up all along the line. Our attack is to start on the right, near Laffaux, we will advance only when ordered.

News arrives at 9. It seems good. In the afternoon, we learn that prisoners number more than 3,000, that Vaudesson and Allemant are in our hands.

In the evening we continue our reconnaissance in the rain. We can't take much more. Dazed, we only desire one thing—to attack so as to get it all over with quicker.

24 October

Today—Victory. After a heavy artillery bombardment at 11 a.m., supported by gas, we receive the order to advance. We capture in succession the Elfes and Cocotier trenches, then the Ravine of Ailleval. The Boches flee and we follow hot on their heels. What a terrain! It's frightful, everything is devastated, we stumble into huge craters, German corpses everywhere, blown to pieces, others overcome by gas, dying. It's dreadful, but superb. The guns thunder in the distance, the battle is ours, for the moment.

25 October

Frenzy, the Boches are in full flight. It's hard to hold the men back, they want to pursue them. But we have done our job; the 5th Battalion replaces us to continue the advance in the direction of Pinon.

At 6 p.m. we leave for the rear, without any relief. Are we going to get some rest at last?

1 November

I get ten days' leave.

[From 13 November 1917 to April 1918 Captain Desagneaux is posted to the Somme, then to the Mailly Camp and finally to Alsace. At the end of March 1918 he finds himself back at the Somme, supporting the British.]

1918

The Somme
1 to 29 April

6 April

Quartered at Laversines, near Beauvais.

The Boches are attacking *en masse*, we are dispatched in haste to the front. And, as we advance, so the zone gets worse; poor refugees of all ages; tramping the road, with tears in their eyes carrying what they can, a few clothes, some chickens or rabbits; sometimes followed by a few cattle.

It's misery on the march.

Laversines is teeming with cavalry, artillery, convoys, vehicles. It's complete and utter chaos, difficult to move around. The locality is full of people who are fleeing from the front, we can't find any billets and have to sleep in ruins, cellars, or in the open air.

7 April

We start to learn what happened during the attack; the civilians who fled from this zone, claim that the English gave way and that, in several places, for distances of 10 kilometres there was absolutely nothing to stop the enemy. If the Germans didn't pass, it's because they didn't dare take the risk, fearing an ambush.

It was our troops, yet again, who saved the situation. Everything they had within reach was thrown into the fray to bridge the gap.

At 9 p.m. arrives an order for us to leave by car tomorrow morning. But then, the height of madness, they take one car per company away from us. The Colonel leaves baggage behind and the commander too. Everyone is ordered to travel lighter—it's liquidation stations. Shouts, cries, gestures. The Ordnance Officer is liquidating his stocks too. When in camp, one had to fight to get a shirt, or underpants, and to get some soap or grease and other indispensables was impossible. Suddenly, fatigue parties bring huge stocks of these. Company Commander, get on with it! You will have one car less, but

1. Henri Desagneaux.

2. Desagneaux's company waiting in reserve in the Bras-Ravin Quarries, Verdun, 17th June 1916.

3. German prisoners leaving a communication trench in the Bras-Ravin Quarries, Verdun, 17th June 1916.

4. The communication trench 'Marie' in the Ravin des Dames, Verdun, during a bombardment, 18th June 1916.

5. Preparing to leave Verdun, 1st July 1916, Desagneaux standing in the centre.

6. Lieutenant Henri Desagneaux leaving the Verdun sector, 2nd July 1916.

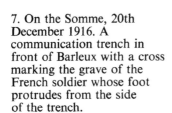

7. On the Somme, 20th December 1916. A communication trench in front of Barleux with a cross marking the grave of the French soldier whose foot protrudes from the side of the trench.

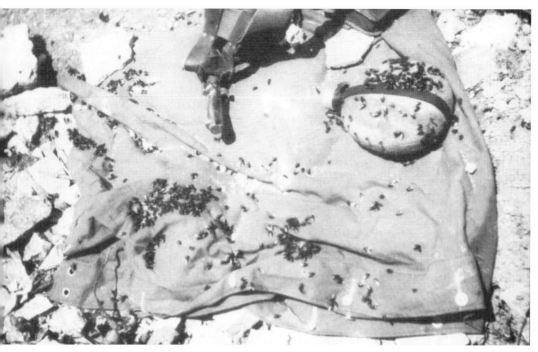

8. Sunshine below Mount Kemmel. See the entry for 21st May 1918.

9. The entrance to a dug-out in the support line at Kemmel, 22nd May 1918. The bodies are all French.

10. The road into Courcelles, 12th June 1918, littered with the bodies of French soldiers.

11. A burial detail at work in Courcelles. The group standing in front of the right-hand building contains two priests, an officer and a medical corpsman.

12. The diarist shaving in a trench in a quiet sector. A sniper's loophole is built into the parapet behind his shoulder and the trenchwork generally is in good condition.

13. An orderly of 359th regiment bringing up the rations—bread, soup, full canteens, coffee, and a bottle of wine.

14. A priest offers Mass behind the lines.

15. The diarist leads his company on a march in a rear area.

here are parcels of underwear, 84 tablets of soap, gas-masks, packets of dressings, equipment, munitions. It doesn't stop coming, the Supply Officer may be better off, but what can I do with all this? The cars are bursting at the seams—the men are so loaded that they can hardly stand and tomorrow we must go.

By the light of our lanterns, we are forced to throw away and waste many of the things which we had so often asked for.

Maps, dozens of them, but no baggage. We are supposed to take everything and yet have nothing with us. Stupid waste. At midnight, the sergeant-majors are still tearing their hair not knowing what to do. They have got piles of mess-tins, dishes, tools, and sacks of material which we won't be able to take with us.

11 April
The Germans continue their attacks: towards the sea: Arras, Ypres, Armentières. The Portuguese, in turn are getting a hiding. We are retreating near Coucy. Everywhere the Boches are attacking, they are gaining ground. The most distressing thing is that when we attack we only manage to advance a few kilometres while they cover 10–12 in one go.

13 April
We leave Argoeuvres at 2.30 a.m. It's a splendid night, there are planes in the sky, fires everywhere, the guns light up the horizon and bombs rend the air, it's superb, but tragic.

Arrival at Raincheval at midday, where we are quartered. The inhabitants are glad to see the French again. They have no confidence in the English any more. During the last Boche attack they lost 25 kilometres; on the first day, regiments—at Amiens—threw down their weapons and fled with the civilians. It is said that they have lost 70,000 men, and 1,100 guns.

8 p.m. Gunfire all the time, the sky is ablaze. There is talk of us leaving at midnight.

People have nothing but praise for the Canadians, Australians, and Hindus—it was they who stopped the enemy advance.

14 April
What a night. We wait in anguish. Sleep is impossible, the guns roar, the houses tremble, even the ground quakes, it's frightful. The weather joins in—rain, gale-force winds, thunder, all the elements are unleashed.

At 1 a.m., order to leave at 2.45. It's Sunday and, half-asleep, we set off again.

The night is pitch black, so that visibility is less than 20 centimetres.

It's a hard task to get the men together, we look for them everywhere while they themselves search for their squads; the road is crawling with soldiers calling each other; in the dead of the night we leave without knowing if everyone is there.

Soaked to the skin we stumble on, like machines, minds blank, while the cannons fire tons of shells in the distance.

At 7 a.m. we arrive at Pas-en-Artois where we are quartered. The inhabitants are glad to see the French again, they have lost confidence in the English. During the last attack, they saw them arriving panic-stricken, having fled 15 kilometres, shouting 'Run for it, run for it', dumping their weapons and ammunition, creating thus a stampede among the civilians. The Boches had nothing in front of them except a horde of refugees; they didn't dare advance too far, that is what saved us.

Everyone says the same: the English are hopeless, it's the Scots, the Australians, and Canadians who do all the work.

It's Sunday, we are in a state of alert. The weather is cold. What is there to do? I look for a bale of straw and go to sleep.

25 April
Alert at dawn. We are off to Coigneux to take up positions in case of attack.

At 6.30 p.m. we return. Our route is scattered with huge English camps, teeming with vehicles, men, and horses. But these men are more interested in polishing and shining their equipment than in thinking about the trenches.

28 April
I receive a personal note from the Colonel. I have been made captain adjutant-major in the 5th Battalion—adjutant to Major Constantin.

I leave my 6th Battalion with regret, and especially my 21st Company where the men were always ready to sacrifice themselves for me. With them, I felt sure that they would not give in and, whatever happened, would not leave me behind.

Well, one must follow one's destiny. The 5th Battalion does not possess a famous reputation and I know hardly anyone in it.

Belgium: Kemmel Sector
29 April to 3 June

5 May

We leave Watou at 1.30 a.m.; the artillery fire is enough to drive one mad. We are now in the firing zone and we pass huge English howitzers, one after the other. The gunners are ramming their shells home like a baker thrusting bread into an oven. The shells go off with a deafening roar and this continues for hours upon end, sometimes their departure coincides with enemy arrivals and there is an almighty spray of fire and earth. We take cover and then move off again. What a march in such an avalanche of fire and by night too! The companies advance half a platoon at a time; we repeatedly come across convoys of artillery trapped in the mud and dead horses blocking the road.

Progress is difficult, our hearts are beating at the thought of what is to come.

Eventually we arrive near Reninghelst, in front of Mount Kemmel where we camp. We will be obliged to wait until evening to effect the relief!

Relief, what a terrible destruction there must be in such a sector, in this deluge of shells! It's one of those sectors where the relief is accomplished—as at Verdun or in the Chemin des Dames—only after 50 to 60 per cent losses.

The 27th Infantry Division, which was at Kemmel when the Boches attacked, has had many of its men taken prisoner; the 154th which was beside it, was wiped out; it's our turn to march now.

At 9 a.m. we leave to reconnoitre our positions; the terrain is unrecognizable, it is merely holes and muddy quagmires, with wrecked vehicles and a jumble of equipment everywhere: devastation, abominable desolation. Up front, none or very few communication trenches. We can't go any further. From the very first battalion we see in reserve, there is nothing but scared soldiers, huddled in shell-holes, not daring to raise their heads. If this is what it's like in reserve, what is it in the front line? There can be no thought of going there in daylight, the artillery fire is continuous and, further on, their machineguns are sweeping our positions with bullets.

We leave without seeing anything. The afternoon is spent in chatting about the coming relief, everyone wondering how he will get out alive. The sector is the sole topic of conversation: we shall only be relieved after a 60 per cent loss of troops; the men are beginning to wish for, not death, but just to be wounded so that they can get out as soon as possible. This leads to endless suppositions; one man gives up his hand, another his arm, provided it's the left one; yet another goes as far as a leg, declaring that where he comes from men like this manage quite well. But what frightens them most, is being wounded in the stomach or some other vital organ. Then the conversation turns to the ambulance, the hospital, plans for convalescence, rest at home, and what to do so as not to return to the front.

In every sort of sector like this, the conversation revolves around the same topic. There is no longer even any mention of the civilians and their cosy life. No, you are stuck there waiting, simply trying to snatch some part of yourself from death, you don't even ask to escape unharmed, it seems too impossible, your only wish is to leave as little as possible of yourself behind on the battlefield.

And then, sometimes a glimmer of hope returns. Haven't we already been through similar sectors and we are still here aren't we! There is talk of the attack; but in an attack, not everyone survives. We run through the list of our comrades left dead at Champagne, at Verdun, on the Chemin des Dames, at La Royère, and Vauxhaillon and, considering their percentage, we conclude that we have perhaps a chance of getting out alive. Yes, but then we'll have to start all over again, and will luck be indefinitely on our side to protect us?

At 6.30 p.m. we proceed to relieve the left sector of Mount Kemmel. Our advance is difficult as there are no communication trenches, just shell craters for our protection. We move forward with a lump in our throats; the shells rain down in front of us, but there's no going back, we have to get through. Our only desire is reach our goal as quickly as possible. A moment's pause, then we are off again. There are explosions on the right, left, everywhere. Sometimes a man stops, wounded; we don't even bother about him, it's such a common occurrence. On we go, knowing full well that he will manage to get to the first-aid post. If his wound is only slight he is envied—he's safe. We advance, the bombardment is heavier, our ranks become thinner, night has fallen, we can't see each other any more, but now and again sheaves of fire bring a sinister gleam to this chaotic terrain.

At last, there's the battalion to be relieved. We shelter in a hole and get our breath. We are in reserve. No dug-outs, nothing, except a simple communication trench which will protect us from shell splinters and that's all. Information is quickly passed on, and after grumbling about the time spent here, their losses, and wishing us good luck, the others take their leave.

What is there to do now but wait, wait and see what happens?

6 May

What a night. It's an orgy of gunfire. The English artillery and ours shoot away. The Boches return the fire, the sky is ablaze. Curled up small and huddled together in our shell-holes we are sprayed with earth and blinded by searing flashes of light. Then, towards midnight, just when the food is due to arrive, gas is unleashed upon us. It's enough to drive you mad. While the distribution of the food is being organized, all masks have to be put on, smoke fills the glasses and we can't see anything any more. We spend hours like this suffocating with parched throats, not daring to take the stifling masks off. During the night, the fatigue parties, which are not familiar with the sector, get lost and we have to go and look for them. Shells burst everywhere. When we do, at last, get the food, the air is full of gas, and we can't take our masks off and the food becomes uneatable.

That night, we have 200 men gassed and evacuated in the 120th Corps, about a similar number in the 297th and in the 359th as well. The loss of relief troops is calculated and the chiefs are struck by the high number of evacuees; the men are accused of having taken their masks off in order to be evacuated. As a result, we get threatening notes from them.

It's Sunday, and there is already talk of us attacking to improve our front-line positions. It's raining. The terrain, the soil of which is clay, is awful. We are eating, sleeping, living in filthy slime.

No shelters, no protection whatsoever. We can't wash, change or sleep. The water gets into everything, it's one almighty quagmire.

7 May

Night falls and with it a frightful bombardment starts up again. To avoid the disorder experienced the previous evening in the provisioning of the troops, I am chosen to take charge this evening. The mobile kitchens come as far as Reninghelst where the fatigue parties meet them. There are few sectors that I have seen where the rear is so heavily shelled. The Boches fire away; the gun batteries, the crossroads, the surrounding countryside are submerged in fire. You don't know where to put yourself, it's madness to try to distribute food in such conditions.

This operation—at night—takes a good half an hour. Midnight, the fatigue parties are there waiting in the ditch by the roadside; One can guess the frightened look on their faces amid the silence which remains unbroken except for the occasional sh—t, when a shell falls too close for comfort. Then amidst the noise of the guns, we hear the mobile kitchens clanking towards us. Unfortunately, at that moment the road itself is hit by a hail of shells. Fear grips every man present. We have chosen for our fatigue party strong, resourceful fellows who won't let us down on the way. The food has to get through and the bravest are selected. However, amid this avalanche of fire, they curse the Boches and everything around them.

Three kitchens from the battalion arrive; the fourth has been left behind on the way with its two horses killed by the same shell blast. The men run forward to collect the food.

The guns roar and it's just like a rugby scrum there. Over here the 17th Company! Come on the 18th! ... 3rd Squad—5th ... Christ ... bl—dy well do it yourself. The cooks are in a hurry, they don't like being in the lines, the sergeant-majors accompanying the kitchens are not the most courageous. The shells burst on all sides, and we can only recognize each other by their flashes of light. People push, shove, and shout to make themselves heard amid the clatter of pots and pans. Then, all of a sudden, a loud whistle is heard very close, everyone dives for cover, with pans flying in all directions. It's over now, the blast was deafening. Shouts of the wounded: 'Over here quickly, I'm hit.' 'Help me, stretcher-bearers, take me to the first-aid post.' The tussle for food becomes ever more frantic with men shouting and struggling, two men are lying on the ground, one at his last gasp, the other with his leg blown off. Suddenly, yet another terrible explosion directly on a kitchen, the horses are killed, the men scatter, some shouting, others groaning, others running for their lives.

Come on, get on with it! The distribution of the food is now carried out in total darkness, with us standing in pools of blood. Blood from the horses, blood from the wounded, they mingle together and the din of the shells is frightful. Then the news goes round: Sergeant-Major Bonnet has been killed. He's from the 17th. It's panic-stations. Command is impossible, the shells burst all around us. Every man has only one idea—to grab what he needs to get away—coffee, the 3rd, wine the 5th, what about your bread, you silly beggars!

'Letters over here', shouts the post orderly who has just arrived.

'Make sure you bring the dishes back', shouts the cook. Everyone is shouting at once, the corporals are assembling their men, some have left, others have taken cover, still more are stretched out never to get up again.

It's raining, and the mud makes the spectacle even sadder. It's barbarous, you can't describe it. The guns are firing still more fiercely; we are here; it's our duty, provisioning is one of the hardest fatigues to do.

The men are now laden like mules, as they have to carry the share of those who have been wounded. The sergeant-majors hurry them along, two kitchens have no horses, they will have to be fetched before dawn.

The shells continue to wreak havoc; more wounded for the first-aid posts; while the two unscathed kitchens rattle back to where they came from, the men, cursing and swearing, disappear into the night to carry the food to their comrades. They will have something to say to them: 'What a time they gave us— the pigs—So you think that it is a cushy job to do?'

I return to my shell-hole, dazed by the noise, with the vision of those poor devils lying wounded on the roadside. Will someone simply take them away? There are so many of them every day!

8 May

Gunfire the whole night long. At 4.15 a.m. our attack is unleashed. We don't know what is supposed to happen. We have simply been told to stand by and be ready for anything. The 359th attacks with two companies. The 15th Infantry Regiment attacks on this flank to the left, while on the right the 297th, followed by the cavalry, advances.

At the same time as we were launching our offensive, the Germans attacked the English division which was helping the 15th. The English give way and a battalion of the 15th is hard-pressed. The situation seeming none too brilliant, we receive the order to prepare a counter-attack. The hours pass slowly and anxiously by. We are in a perpetual state of alert. Towards evening, with gas shells falling all round us, we are forced to put on our masks and are virtually suffocated for hours on end.

At 8 p.m. we learn that on the left our position has been re-established. This means rest for the time being. How long will it last?

9 May

The artillery has been quieter this evening. The sun rises. We learn the news of yesterday's attacks. It's not very good.

Our two companies encountered the Boches and took ten prisoners. But Roulleau, in charge of the 38th, was killed; Chautrier, commanding the 39th, has been reported missing with two platoons from his company. The troops were forced back to their former positions.

The 297th did not enjoy any greater success.

We'll start again, that's for sure. But why these unco-ordinated paltry little attacks by two or three companies from different battalions attacking each one for its own sake?

Today it was Viset's company's turn to attack and occupy 'Le Pompier', a former café, now in ruins, 500 metres up the hill. They were stopped in their tracks, scythed down by machine-gunfire. What's the use of these attacks in such a sector?

At 9 p.m. we depart to relieve the support battalion at La Clytte, in front of Mount Kemmel. What a crazy relief it is. We leave and cross the tiny village with no means of protection, led by a guide who doesn't know his way. The artillery has opened up again and shells splatter us with mud at every step. We advance sliding and slithering in thick slimy mud; with only one desire—to get there. But no one knows the way, the gunfire makes us do a detour and we get caught up in old barbed-wire entanglements. With our clothes and flesh torn to ribbons, they bombard us with gas, which, half-blinded and choking, slows up our advance. Miraculously no one in our column is wounded; but it's not the same story for the rest of the battalion.

Now, we have arrived at our command post which is one in name rather than in appearance.

It's a former artillery look-out post, which wouldn't resist a 105. Inside it's one huge puddle of slimy mud and water; they have placed a duckboard in the middle. We have to shelter in here with all the communications personnel, there's room for six, and we are at least thirty. In our post, it's so horrible that you just don't know where to put your wet muddy feet and yet we shall have to live and sleep in here for days on end.

11–13 May

Still in a state of alert, we are awaiting events. The artillery is as active as ever.

On the 13th at 5 a.m., I leave at dawn to reconnoitre the front line. It's no different from any other; artillery fire, and as you get closer the whistle of machine-gun bullets, you can't see a thing in these sort of reconnaissances. One has to be on the spot to really know the sector. The gas has made me very tired; I move with difficulty and on my return journey the guns seem to be pursuing me. With Pierre my orderly, jumping from hole to hole, we finally reach our post under heavy fire. The major, who had been watching our return, heaves a sigh of relief at our safe arrival, as the shells spare no metre of ground. We await once again the shell which will hit our shelter and explode amongst us. Every burst seems nearer! While sheltering in bomb-craters, several of our men are hit and come, streaming with blood to seek refuge with us; for several hours, it's nothing but blood and groans until the poor devils can go and get their wounds dressed at nightfall.

At 10 p.m. we set out to relieve the front line battalion which is before La Clytte. We haven't got a lot of ground to cover, but as it has been raining the terrain is slippery and battered by ceaseless artillery fire. We get caught up in telephone wires, it's a real nightmare.

14 May

What a sector. We are on a hill top—the main target of the German guns. At the bottom of the hill, two companies; near the railway line—one company in reserve with us. No trenches—only holes.

With the coming attack in mind, the artillery officers proceed to adjust their guns; but they refrain from going to the front lines, preferring to do their job with binoculars.

At nightfall, I go and reconnoitre the front lines near the railway line. One can easily get lost in this place as there are no communication trenches and no landmarks.

The companies are scattered here and there, anywhere they could find some holes to shelter in. There is no communication between them. From time to time, I come across clusters of corpses, remnants of previous attacks which have not been able to be removed. They are stinking, but when I try to escape them, I merely stumble across more. Grim battlefield where in a few days we shall be fighting in our turn. The German artillery shoots incessantly, and gas shells fall at our feet. With our masks on once again, breathing heavily and half-suffocated, Pierre and I return to our command post.

15 May

1 a.m.—gas again, our shelter is full of it. You can hardly breathe, your throat burns; you cough and spit, tears stream down your face. There can be no thought of sleep. The guns are firing madly, we are in a state of alert as we expect to be attacked at dawn.

However, the morning passes uneventfully, can we now doze off a little? Our orders for the coming attack arrive, the terrain has to be studied, and from 4 p.m., the Boches bombard us, firing gas-shells as well.

Our losses increase daily; about 200 per battalion, i.e. 600 for the regiment. Life is getting harder: no sleep, we are wallowing in mud and filth. We can neither wash nor lie down except on the ground itself and there is not a wisp of straw; our joints are stiff and we are itching all over.

18 May

I receive precise details of the attack: I have been designated to command a communication detachment between the 121st Infantry Division on the left and ours. In my command, one infantry company and one company of machine-gunners, half taken from the 359th and the other from the neighbouring regiment. It's an awful job, as I will not know the troops placed under me until the very last moment. The attack is for the 20th. The men are exhausted, effectives are reduced to 60 or 70 per company, there are no N.C.O.s and they have been in the sector for fifteen days already.

19 May

The attack is for tomorrow morning; I go and inspect the terrain. The starting point has been fixed at the railway embankment in the ravine. My objective, a nameless farm. We shall have to cross the railway line, then the small stream at Kemmelbeck and then climb a slope. If we get there, I am supposed to hold my position, withstand enemy fire with no shelter of any kind and resist any counter-attacks until relief arrives.

It's a day full of anguish. Orders and counter-orders flood in. You don't know what to believe. Being thus responsible to the 121st Infantry Division for the attack, I am sent to Reninghelst to see a major who has nothing to do with me, whereas the one who will be in charge of the attack is still at Poperinghe and will only arrive at the lines this evening.

It's utter confusion. And it's Sunday. Whit Sunday. Marvellous weather, not a cloud, brilliant sunshine, and tonight we shall have to go to our deaths. We would love to banish all our hopes and fears until afterwards.

What sadness there is in our shelter rocked by shell-fire. What hope is there? You can't always go on without copping it, won't the fatal moment come when our luck will turn? And while we are here waiting to die, others have been relaxing for the past four years in the rear, or in some headquarters, or in a driving seat! All those fine army circulars have not succeeded in ousting them. Even in the camp up front, there are some who have been vegetating there for one or two years; it's always the same ones who are sent and when reinforcements arrive, it's those who were wounded a few days previously who return, whilst so many others who are fit and capable have never seen a trench and don't know what a shell-burst is.

The hours pass, night spreads its dark cloak over the huge field whilst the artillery pounds the lines and the rear.

The latest orders arrive. I transmit mine; two platoons in line, each with a squad of machine-gunners; as a second wave of attack, two platoons each of infantry and machine-guns. Plans for wiping out the enemy trenches, organization of our position.

Dinner? We aren't hungry, our throats are dry, our only thoughts are of what is to come. The major stays at his post, a hand-shake before leaving, a 'good luck' and I disappear into the night with Pierre—towards the great unknown.

20 May

Whit Monday. Splendid evening; the stars are shining in the sky, and on the ground shells burst in sheets of light.

At midnight, I make my way to the point where I am supposed to meet the company from the 36th Infantry Regiment which has been placed under my command. I have no information concerning the officers and N.C.O.s in it and I shall have to lead an attack with troops that I have never seen before.

At 1 a.m. the troops arrive at their position near the railway-line; then we notice that we are totally unprotected and that there isn't enough room for everyone. How dismal it is to watch in the darkness these files of men, bent in two, silently groping for some spot to shelter in. They jostle one another, each man trying to recognize his neighbour—they are soon forced to spread along the railway line towards the right. But they fall upon a mound of corpses, remnants from previous attacks; the stench is vile. Through the darkness we perceive shapeless forms, legs folded in two, arms outstretched, eyes wide open. The whole place is littered with bodies, weapons, and equipment; the smell forces us back. We can't think of staying there, the men must be moved away so they are spared this vision of death before confronting it themselves.

Therefore, we fall back towards the left; there will be a gap on our right. Each man digs, as best as he can, a hole to prevent himself from being seen. But aren't we digging our own graves in the night?

At last, we are in position, time ticks by, and dawn is about to break. The officers from the 36th come to discuss the attack with me, their orders don't coincide with mine. Their order is to launch the attack at 3 minutes to 6, whilst we are due to attack at 6. What a confabulation! Everyone is trying to save his own skin and to find some means of escape. Tired of talking, I order them to obey my commands. Then, something else, the foot-bridges which are to help us cross the Kemmelbeck are not there, the bright spark who was supposed to put them there has found it easier not to bother. What organization! Everyone is trying to protect himself and acts just as he pleases—the generals are far away aren't they? No cohesion. Poor soldier? Here's your orders and—get on with it!

3.30 a.m., at last the day breaks and puts an end to all indecision. Mount Kemmel towers darkly above us and up in the sky the planes begin their inspection. We are forced to take cover.

4 a.m. It's dawn now—we are in a state of anguish, the planes are 50 metres above us, the weather is exceptionally clear, it's just not possible that they don't see us. We curl up even smaller, we would burrow into the ground if we could. Not a murmur, except for the drone of the planes which circle tirelessly above us. They are flying so low that at any moment we expect to see a flare go up which will alert their artillery. Then we will be horribly crushed.

5.15. Not a sound: you would think that both artilleries came to some agreement this morning so as to destroy us better later on.

5.30. Final recommendations between comrades: If I fall, you won't leave me there—my packet of bandages is here—you've got my family's address, you know whom to tell.

5.40. Sad at heart, everyone looks at his watch, a few minutes and it will be time to go. A last mouthful of wine or rum to give oneself some courage, a few final preparations, we adjust our belts and cartridge-pouches.

5.45. Calm and deathly silence, what is our artillery doing that it is not pounding away at the Boches? God, how long the minutes are!

5.50. Suddenly, as if by magic, the barrage is unleashed. It's unbelievable: 75s, 90s, 110s, 155s, all firing at once. Shells of every sort shower down in their thousands in front of us. It's just one curtain of smoke, we can't see a thing any more. Behind us, a gun is firing 75s at 8 metres on Butterfly Farm. The din is frightful. The Boches do not return the fire. It's such a beautiful sight that everyone comes out of his hole to watch.

5.56–57. Make ready! With a lump in our throats, and no more time for thought we concentrate on the hands of our watch which has been set for 5.58.

Bayonets fixed. Amid the noise of gunfire, orders echo along the line. Stand by to attack.

6 a.m. Forward, forward. Everyone is on his feet, we join up with the others, we're off. We stick as close to our barrage as possible, on occasions too closely, some of our men are wounded by our own shells. We curse it for not moving forward quickly enough. We would like to be up there already before the Boches start firing.

Suddenly, machine-gun bullets whistle past us; the Boches are on to us. We take cover, then move off again. The barrage moves on, and we follow. Our only thought is to advance, to reach our goal. We are stopped momentarily at the Kemmelbeck stream—no gangplanks.

We push and shove, then flounder in water up to our thighs; we've crossed it. Getting wet doesn't matter, we must advance, reach the ridge which draws nearer and nearer, at any price. Bullets hiss over our heads again, some wounded limp back to the rear; nobody pays them any attention, all our attention is focused on the ridge.

The barrage lengthens again, and falls beyond the ridge to pound the rear of the enemy's lines. Then, panic-stricken, a group of Boches comes stumbling down, without weapons or equipment, and with their hands in the air. They seem half-crazed, with their eyes bulging out of their heads, our barrage has stunned them. We are at the ridge. There are German corpses there, chunks of bloody flesh, with terror written on their faces which are almost black already.

On we go, we are over the ridge, the nameless farm is ours. Spades out, and while everyone is digging away, flinging to one side the evil-smelling corpses, I install my machine-guns and organize communications and positions.

We recapture 4 British guns abandoned here during a previous attack. We take in addition 4 machine-guns and 18 Boches.

We take cover, Mount Kemmel looks down on us; the reaction of the Boches promises to be terrible. In front of us, it's a plain as far as the foot of Mount Kemmel, no protection anywhere.

Our success is total. The sun is resplendent. We can breathe at last.

7 a.m. We shall have to spend the complete day in this spot, in a hole a few centimetres across, not moving for fear of giving ourselves away. The prospect of being relieved makes it bearable.

10 a.m. The Boches react. Our reserves are showered with shells. While awaiting our turn, we hurry to get all our organization complete. We dig, dig, and dig. The heat is torrid, the corpses are giving off an awful stench. We should really have a bite to eat. Pierre lost the food we had sometime during the advance, so we have to make do with a piece of chocolate—still we haven't got much appetite. The Boches really do stink too much and their shells are getting closer.

There can be no hope of getting some sleep in such heat. We wait and scratch. Everyone looks for his fleas and every time he discovers one, crushing it between his finger-nails gives him a sense of moral relief. It seems that he will scratch less now.

We await relief without knowing whether it will come. It is the main hope and topic of all our conversations. Everyone surmises on the direction he will take to escape the baggage of fire. Some decide to go in a straight line, even if it means crossing old barbed-wire entanglements, others will wait and see what the evening has to offer.

We wait, and in front of us Mount Kemmel rises formidably. It seems that all German eyes are upon us, we don't dare get up or move. Every time a man moves out of his hole to satisfy the call of nature voices call him back and make him keep his head down: Are you crazy, you silly b—, you'll get us spotted, you numbskull.'

The afternoon passes without mishap—but relief is not forthcoming, everyone is glum again; they have bitter words for those who leave them here. 'Are the pigs going to leave us to die here like dogs? Perhaps they imagine that we haven't done enough already! Twenty-four hours here, I'm fed up. And our food? Who is going to bring it? Nobody here will hear of doing 6 or 7 kilometres and as many back again to go and fetch it! Ah the pigs!'

While these insults fly, evening falls and the artillery open up. Soon we are in an inferno of fire; at La Clytte everything is ablaze and in the fields the former English barrack huts and some ruined farms are in flames. Munition dumps explode, it's a real firework display. The whole plain is alight, it's war in all its horror.

Huge shells rain down in the ravine and on the railway track, forming a virtually impenetrable wall. We tremble at the thought of having to cross this area during the relief.

The Boches are jumpy and start firing at the least pretext. We, too, fear a counter-attack and our artillery is on edge.

Amid this fury of projectiles, neither food nor orders can reach us. We are separated from the world.

In front our baggage, behind us the Boches. Our water bottles are getting empty. We sparingly keep a few drops for tomorrow, thinking of the wounded or of the heat.

As for food, no one is hungry and a bar of chocolate or a tin of bully beef will be ample.

How long the night's wait seems! There is no thought of rest, we work frantically. Crouched in our hole we await a lull in the barrage so that we can dig our hole deeper for tomorrow. Next we rid ourselves of the foul-smelling German bodies by flinging them as far away as possible; everyone works until the guns start firing more violently again.

21 May

Night draws to its close and day is about to break. We are hoping for some respite. Suddenly, as well as the violent explosions which splatter us with earth, we have to contend with gas shells which give off a noxious white vapour. 'Gas, gas'—the cry echoes all along the line. We shall have to live with our masks on, and be prepared for a counter-attack.

It's a glorious day, a real warm spring morning, it's going to be hot later on. Planes fly over both lines, and the artillery holds its fire for fear of being spotted. We would be able to get a breath of fresh air, if it were not for the German planes buzzing about above us, taking piles of photographs. Mount Kemmel has its eyes on us too, we have to curl up as small as possible so as not to be seen. We wait and we scratch. We are living in the earth, our clothes are thick with dirt, we are itching all over, in our shoes, in our trousers, under our shirts we can't even nod off for one single moment. Even if the guns are silent, the bugs keep on crawling.

God, how filthy we are! Fifteen days' growth of beard, and for the last eighteen days I haven't taken my shoes off or had a change of underwear. We have no water to wash in, just mud all around us. We can't even satisfy the call of nature any more. Mount Kemmel is ever-present, watching, and we are forced to wait until nightfall, unless we want our heads blown off.

Our thoughts turn to the coming relief and to the long hard road back to get away from all this.

As soon as evening falls, the artillery fire becomes intense and draws ever closer. The Boches must have brought some new guns up into action. Smoke and flames billow from our lines in the rear, and our former position at La Clytte. In the ravine below us and on the railway track, huge 210s and 150s explode with a deafening roar.

A little later at 9.30 p.m., while I was inspecting the lines and making final preparations for the relief which we were told would come tonight, the first barrage opens up. Despite its horror, the cry is unanimous—it's superb. La Clytte is in flames, munition dumps explode, Mount Kemmel is one huge ball of smoke.

Ah, what a pounding the Boches are getting—yes, but we are getting one too. It's one barrage of fire everywhere and the Boches are pouring gas upon us. For the fifteenth or twentieth time of the day, we put our masks on.

We await our relief. Can it take place, will the soldiers be able to cross this wall of metal and flames to reach us? The relief is due at midnight. It is 11 p.m. and the guns rage.

All of a sudden, a shout in front of us: 'The Boches, the Boches.' It's a counter-attack. At one and the same time, machine-guns open up, rifles fire at point-blank range, grenades explode everywhere and as soon as a red flare is up, our barrage starts up. The Boches suffer heavy losses and those who can escape do so in disorder.

22 May

Midnight. The barrage stops, but there is still heavy firing on the rear and on the lines; we are in a cloud of smoke. The shells burst 2 or 3 metres from us. Not a drop of water to drink, our throats are parched, we wait. Crash! We are covered with earth. That one's not ours. We await the next. In the hole next to us two men are buried. Help me! One of them runs for it, crazed with fear; another has a broken leg. He's nothing to help him except his packet of dressings. Carry him to safety?—We can't even think of it in such a hail of fire. Crash! It's

still not our turn, but again, there are cries of agony from a neighbouring hole. Are we all going to be wiped out one by one before
being relieved? Relief, we've never given up thinking about it. How
could one get through such a furnace alive? Isn't it better to stay
where we are?

A priest with a team of stretcher-bearers has come by night to bury
the dead. Ah, he may as well have stayed where he was. This team is
dispirited, it would like to be far away, they are bandsmen who don't
like life in the infantry.

Our relief is overdue, the gunfire seems even heavier. It's the 6th
and 10th Battalions who are supposed to be coming to relieve the
36th Infantry Battalion on my left, the Desagneaux detachment and
the 5th Battalion. It's my job to place the battalion which is relieving
the 5th and my detachment.

At 1.15 a.m. some men arrive, half-crazed; they have lost their
leader, and have left many comrades killed or wounded on the way.
They don't know if the others have been able to get through nor
whom they must relieve.

Time passes, no one—and the guns fire incessantly, throwing up a
huge wall of fire in the ravine and on the railway-line.

1.45 a.m., no-one comes.

2 a.m. A platoon arrives now, commanded by a sergeant who has
no idea of the company he is supposed to relieve. Time is pressing,
dawn comes early, and with it disappears our hope of leaving.

I put this squad in position, the previous one runs away.

2.15. Nothing.

2.30. Nothing.

At 2.35 a sergeant and two corporals arrive, their men have been
left on the way, terrified by the gas or artillery-fire, wounded or
killed.

Daylight will soon be here, will we be able to get through when our
turn comes? The enemy artillery is battering the railway track and the
ravine. I send some men to look for our units. We shall have to
hurry.

2.45. Some more men arrive. The relief is taking place as best it can,
the units will group together later on.

3 a.m. One company on the right has now been relieved; my detachment has left in turn.

3.10. The last company is complete. We all leave in small groups.

3.15. Day breaks. I give a last-minute report which is very brief:

our lines are from here to there, the position of our machine-guns, enemy positions, hold your ground!

3.30. It only remains for me to go now. Alas, do the Boches fear an attack? But there's a real barrage of 150s and 210s on the railway, smoke everywhere, you can't see a thing beyond it, except for the peak of La Clytte where German shells are exploding.

We are ready—Pierre and I—we anxiously look for a gap which would allow us through. Nothing but smoke. Yet we have to go, let's try the quietest spot, and we'll see as we go. We leave, and we haven't gone 100 metres when we meet the first French body, fallen during tonight's relief. Poor devil with his face crushed, arms outstretched, there's nothing we can do for him. On we go, and all the way we come across wounded making for the rear, or piles of corpses, in fours and fives, no longer red, but black, decomposing on the spot—What an awful sight! Naked, limbs twisted, with sometimes a leg lying on its own covered in blood. We have to step over these bodies, across a maze of holes, strewn with the foul-smelling corpses of men and horses; the ground reeks of gunpowder and gas. The smell gets down into your throat, but there can be no stopping now, the firing seems to be dying down, it's time to cross the railway line, we are running now, calling upon every bit of strength we have left. We're across the ravine, we've got the slope and the peak of La Clytte to cross.

Finally we arrive at the trenches at La Clytte. There's hardly anything left of the dugouts and trenches. Some heads pop up, 'For Christ's sake, hide, you are going to get us spotted'—the eternal fear of the front-line soldier. The entrance to the battalion command post has been blocked by a shell, three bodies lay there in a pool of blood; once more we can't find our way. A voice from underground calls out to us, it's the major who has seen us passing. We join him. It was about time! Scarcely are we inside when a broadside of shells makes the ground shake around us.

I'm exhausted, my throat is parched, the major gives me a drink and after his congratulations, I sink into a deep sleep. It's almost 5 a.m.

At 6, Pierre wakes me. The major is leaving, the guns have quietened a little—it's time to make a dash for it. We make our positions at Zevecotten where we spend the day. We can breathe a little now, the worst is over. It would be real bad luck if, after escaping out of this furnace, we were to cop it now.

The weather is glorious, we can get some fresh air, without having to keep our heads down. Tomorrow, we'll have water and I shall be able to shave and change my clothes. Oh, just to take off my shirt, and to get rid of these ever-increasing fleas, not to scratch any more! And then not to have to eat chocolate or jam or some tasteless tinned food. And sleep! What a prospect. But for the moment, I can't keep still, I just don't stop scratching.

23 May

At 2 a.m. the relieving troops arrive. We set off at full speed. There's Reninghelst to be crossed. Shells fall near us from time to time, but what does it matter, we are gaining ground and in front of us, is our rear! Our only thought is to put as much distance as possible between ourselves and the enemy, tiredness doesn't count any more.

At dawn we see along our route the last of our guns firing relentlessly, surrounded by huge piles of shells, dead horses, and smashed wagons. We hurry to get out of range.

Abeele at last, where we camp, the guns can't reach us here. We don't stay here long and at 2 p.m. there is motorized transport waiting for us.

We drive on and on and as the kilometres scurry by, smiles return to our faces, we feel alive again. Over there the guns are thundering but we aren't there any more. The devastated landscape is replaced by an inhabited one: one civilian, two civilians—joy. A whistle, it's the railway, people, life is beginning again. In the evening, we get off at Malo-les-Bains. Not many people here, the houses are shuttered up, no one in the streets. This area is frequently bombed by German planes and shelled by long-range artillery and a large number of the civilian population have fled.

But we've got a room, a bed, and some water. The first job will be to have a wash, then to get some sleep.

They say that we will only be here for forty-eight hours, enough time to get ourselves cleaned up, then we will go by train to a spot where we can have a rest. Yes, that's just what we need, we are still too near the lines here; we must leave the enemy as far behind as possible.

24–25–26 May

The bad weather returns, rain the whole day, the sea is grey. Spit and polish, groups gather and everyone has his word to say. Each has done more than his neighbour, has captured his Boche and performed some fine deed in battle.

Fine weather again, I make the most of it by going for a swim every morning. The water is not very warm, but it's so nice not to feel oneself a soldier any more.

Our orders are to walk about, to get some fresh air. For once, there is no talk of exercises, we organize concerts while the generals arrange parades. We stroll around, most people making for the beach which is lined with barbed wire—it's rest for once.

The generals come and mix with the men, it's such a long time since we saw them, and hand round packets of tobacco and cigarettes. Things would be perfect if it were not for the beastly temper of the Colonel, which is worse because everyone appears to be happy. He is as cross as two sticks, he won't admit that some men deserve a decoration. Did he see anything crouching there in his shelter, never leaving it for fifteen days?

We refuse to accept this, but have to struggle hard to obtain ten ribbons a company. Why should one have to bargain in such a way on behalf of men who are always ready to do what is demanded of them?

My losses have been numerous, in the regiment 11 officers and 700 men (in my battalion 5 officers and 260 men).

Our state of health leaves a lot to be desired; we all more or less reek of gas, we have absorbed so much of it. Every day there are new cases reported, and the doctors evacuate them with bronchitis and conjunctivitis.

In the hospitals there have been several deaths announced.

The days go by. Leave is granted, but only a few at a time, to avoid complaints.

29 May
Huge parade on the beach, decoration ceremony.

Reinforcements arrive, we refill our ranks and reform. Major Constantin goes on leave, I take command of the 5th Battalion.

Oise Sector
5 June to 9 August
Attack on Courcelles: 11 June

5 June
Campremy. We are now in the region of Montdidier, in the American sector.

At 8 in the evening, great commotion, German planes drop a shower of bombs on our quarters. Sometimes there are five or six bombs exploding at once; many casualties. These planes also take our transport by surprise, a train carrying troops from the 297th is cut in two. Five officers killed, large number of wounded.

The weather is glorious. We miss Malo, the beach, and the expanse of sea.

6 June

Soldiers from Martinique and the 1918 new recruits are brought in to complete the companies' ranks. With these youngsters, we shall be expected to launch an attack before very long.

10 June

4 p.m. Order to proceed in the direction of the enemy near Maignelay, and that's all.

I'm in command of the 5th Battalion. The situation is none too brilliant. We have no idea what's in front of us, nor to our right. The artillery does just what it pleases, and there is a successive flow of orders and counter-orders.

I receive a brief note telling me to form an advance guard, some cavalry troops have been put at my disposal and . . . get on with it!

At nightfall, we arrive at Maignelay; my battalion takes up forward positions in some woods. Pitch black, thick mud, no information, no orders, nothing.

11 June

A 3 a.m., just when the companies are acquainted with their positions and the machine-gunners in place—and with what difficulty in a night as dark as this, I receive an order to return immediately to Maignelay itself and to make my arrangements for an attack.

What does this mean?

Orders succeed each other—everyone has to be regrouped. The men who are half-asleep complain bitterly, they are fed up.

It's so dark that we make little progress, no one recognizing the way. The cooks are hastily alerted. At 5 a.m., coffee is distributed. This makes all the difference, and at 6 a.m. the battalion is assembled on the road to Maignelay.

No orders, I wait.

At 7, the Colonel sends for me. He is very excited and seems tired.

In front of him a map. With a finger he explains that the whole division is going to form at the railway-line near Tricot and at 9.45 proceed to attack Courcelles and Mortemer-Grand Bois. Twenty-four tanks will accompany us to Courcelles where our lines are; the artillery preparation is to last half an hour. Five divisions are co-operating in the attack under the command of General Mangin.

And that's all, nothing on paper, no other explanation—how the regiment is marching, its formation, the position occupied by my battalion, liaison with the right and left, nothing.

The Colonel seems overwhelmed, incapable of anything. Perhaps it's because there, he won't be in his dug-out and will have to accompany us? Scrap by scrap I obtain from him the information I judge indispensable.

The regiment, formed at Tricot behind the railway-track, will advance with the 16th and 10th Battalions in front, the 5th behind the 6th (it was in fact my battalion which was the last one at Mount Kemmel). Deployed formation, liaison on the right with the light infantry (Chasseurs), on the left, nothing: we form the wing. The 297th is in reserve.

Direction: Courcelles, then Mortemer. Time of attack: 9.45.

That's all I can learn. It is 7.30. The regiment leaves Maignelay.

We haven't been able to transmit our orders. The troops don't know what is expected of them. They have heard about the attack, but so what? It's 8 in the morning, the sun is climbing in the sky, one does not attack like this in broad daylight—to attack now? It's just not possible. When we attack normally, we proceed to our starting positions at night, from in the front line, to go over the top at daybreak. But an attack now? Impossible, it's broad daylight and we are far from our lines; the division can't reach the departure point until midday.

Silently, we march on, nevertheless aware of the serious nature of the situation.

Enemy planes circle above, but it's misty and they can't see us.

On our way we come across some artillery officers choosing a site or some who have only just arrived. On seeing this everyone is happier. 'Told you we won't attack, guns aren't even there.' Faces become brighter, but this gaiety doesn't last long.

Can a soldier think for one moment that an attack without artillery is possible in 1918? NO. Then the attack can only possibly take place tomorrow morning. Until then . . . all hopes are permissible.

Time passes however and we arrive at the railway line at Tricot. The two leading battalions are already there, massed behind the track in an indescribable swarm.

Everyone tries to find out what is happening, we transmit our orders to each other. The Colonel is nowhere to be found.

On the way, we shake hands; Ruby, Morel, Picquet, Maupin, Guidicelli. See you later, mates. . . .

Sheltered by a small hedge, I group my battalion in its turn behind the 6th and I assemble my company officers. Order: the regiment is to attack at 9.45. Direction—Courcelles. Proceed towards the church-steeple, in the wake of the 6th Battalion. Important point: don't get stuck in Courcelles itself, but bypass it to the left.

Mounot's and Trillat's companies in front, 500 metres behind the 6th Battalion. One squad of machine-gunners accompanying each company.

Jouvanceau's company in the rear, outflanking towards the left.

I am in the centre of the battalion with the squad of machine-gunners, my communications officers, my telephonists, stretcher-bearers, and grenadiers.

Once a few more detailed orders have been given, we inspect the terrain. The sun is up, the weather is glorious, the heat is going to be torrid.

In front of us, fields, nothing but fields, the corn is high and is a mass of golden ears. War has not passed through here yet.

In the distance 3 or 4 kilometres away, rises the church steeple of Courcelles, surrounded by green countryside and further on the outline of the woods at Rollot and the dark silhouette of Mortemer. Our impression is that, as soon as we cross the railway line, we shall be in full view of the enemy. The terrain is as flat as a billiard table.

We still can't understand an attack in such conditions—it seems utter madness.

But there's no time to palaver, the captains have gone to give their orders, it's 9.45, the regiment sets off noisily.

At this moment the tank officers arrive and put themselves at our disposal. Four tanks are due to accompany my battalion, they will join me at Courcelles.

The 6th and 10th Battalions have left, it's our turn to go now. The companies set off in perfect order. It's wonderful. You would think yourself at manoeuvres.

But scarcely have we crossed the railway when the first shells splatter us with mud and, ahead of us, the leading battalions are submerged in smoke. The enemy has seen our movements, and is firing for all he is worth.

The whole plain is showered with 105s and 150s. We can clearly distinguish three successive barrages. And we have almost 4 kilometres to cover to reach Courcelles, where, only then will we find the French lines.

We think we must be dreaming. Is it possible that they have ordered the division to attack under such conditions?

On we go, however, stopping occasionally to check on the men and to inspect the horizon.

Nobody says a word; in front of us a barrage is throwing up a wall of earth, how will we get through? The sun burns us with its rays, the German planes are above us. It seems such a long time since we left, but much has still to be done.

We are in the thick of the barrage, clods of earth are flying in all directions, fire and smoke swirl around us, we hasten to cross this wall. Swearwords ring out everywhere, men stop, killed or wounded, but there is no stopping, we go on and on, we have to get through at any cost. A shell covers us with mud, we're through, the barrage is behind us.

Pause to get our breath back. We have a quick swig—God, how dry our throats are. Everyone is streaming with perspiration and panting; in front of us, a few hundred metres away, there is another barrage of fire to cross.

Where are the other companies? Trillat's and Mounot's are in front, they are going all right. The company on the flank is also visible in the distance.

We move off again. We have difficulty in advancing through these huge cornfields, and from now on we do nothing but stumble across the wounded. They are abandoned here, amid the tall blades of corn, helpless. Those who can walk, flee towards the rear; those wounded in the leg, the stomach, or even more seriously patch themselves up while waiting for help. Help; when will it come? The regiment has moved on, will they find them in these huge fields, lying among the tall corn? How many are going to end up dying through lack of attention and will rot where they fell!

We advance nevertheless under the burning sun and the fire of the enemy. This firing grows fiercer. We have to cross the trenches of our second and third lines, then barbed-wire entanglements. We climb over them, scratching and tearing our flesh—but on we go, ever faster, the steeple is still some way off, and we must get there.

Second barrage. Halt. Breather, we shall have to get a move on. We are in a cloud of smoke, yet again the earth flies in all directions, the powder blinds us, and the shells make us dive for cover. Shouts, cries, and groans of the wounded, but its forward we go, this is no time to stop. We fall, pick ourselves up, and move off again. We can't see a thing, it's crazy. Yet daylight reappears, the barrage is crossed.

Stop. Quick count of the men—some missing. Impossible to help these poor devils.

The teams of stretcher-bearers are disorganized now, the men have fallen and the stretchers have been abandoned on the way. What will happen further on?

Yet we are still not at our goal, the third barrage is there in front of us waiting!

Ah! to fall there, and not to have to think any more nor to see these devastated fields, the ever-pursuing bullets, the wounded croaking their last, and the dead who have writhed in vain!

Come on, let's cast such thoughts aside, onwards, the steeple is drawing nearer. Soon the village of Courcelles appears in a swirl of smoke, in a hurricane of fire. I would like to shout to my comrades up in front: 'Remember my advice, pass to the left, above all don't go straight into the village.'

Those who fall into this trap will be wiped out. The enemy has concentrated all its fire on to the surrounding area—one can see nothing but smoke, fire, and powder.

10.30. We have been advancing for three-quarters of an hour, the leading companies' lines seem to be wavering, the outlines of the battalions are no longer distinguishable.

The losses must be enormous, how will we reach our goal?

The artillery seems to double in fury, the shells fall like hail—soon the barrage is visible. But what is our artillery doing? We can't hear anything passing over our heads. Are our guns even in place? And what would they fire with? Tiny little 75s, while the Boches are sending us 105s and 150s, and 210s are raining down on Courcelles.

This day seems crazier and crazier. Yet we advance, frightened and worn-out as we are, hastening on, with the idea that the quicker we go the sooner we shall reach our goal. Goal? Who knows what it is? We were told: direction Courcelles, then Mortemer. And then? Do the big chiefs alone know what we are supposed to be doing? Certainly not, for to explain away this day of madness, they are to tell us afterwards that the division was sacrificed, that its mission was to create a diversion, to stop the Boches at any price, to favour an attack by other divisions on Ressons-sur-Matz!

The third barrage stretches in front of us. We have summoned up our last ounce of strength and dash forward, heads down, seeing nothing, hearing nothing, with one idea in our minds; to get through and come out the other side.

There is earth flying in all directions; we are showered with splinters, sulphur, slime; men fall wounded, and suddenly—an enormous pssst! thump! a 150 has embedded itself in the ground beneath our feet. It happened so quickly, that nobody even moved! Everyone thought that this was the end. The noise over, we look at each other—the shell has not exploded!!! We would have died there, ten to fifteen of us, it's unheard of, it didn't explode! We can't believe it, and in spite of the gunfire we all go and gaze at the hole left by the projectile. It's so unbelievable that I feel around for it with my cane, it's there alright, about a metre beneath the ground under our feet. So there's still some hope, our turn won't come today.

Soaked to the skin, streaming with sweat, we move forward; we are through the barrage now. Here is Courcelles waiting for us. It's enveloped in a cloud of fire and smoke. It's indescribable. There are groups of wounded everywhere, making their way towards the rear. At every step, there's a dying man, or one who has just died. What a nightmare—and the attack properly speaking hasn't even begun, we still haven't reached the French lines.

As we approach them, we get caught in machine-gunfire and the bullets whistle around us. At the very moment before reaching our trenches at Courcelles, there's a shout at my side. 'Captain I'm wounded!' Pierre is on the ground, with blood pissing from his foot; he's got a machine-gun bullet in the leg. He can't walk, what can I do? We have lost all our stretcher-bearers, I have no one to carry him, we must keep up the advance.

Yet, he begs me, 'Captain, don't leave me here'. With difficulty, we drag him as far as the trench.

It is 11 a.m. We get our breath back. The tanks are not here yet. Where are the leading battalions? Where are my companies? What has become of the officers and men in this terrible furnace?

Should we carry on? First we ought to regroup and regain some cohesion. The Colonel is nowhere to be seen, and I can't find out a thing. Suddenly, a shout: the tanks! They are big Saint-Chamonds, monstrous masses of iron, rumbling up the road in broad daylight.

What a sight! The Boches concentrate all their guns upon them, it's a deluge of fire. Some are destroyed on the spot, some are set on fire, some stagger along, trying to reach the plain, only to be blown up further on, others succeed in crossing the lines only to be brought to a crushing halt 100 metres later. In a quarter of an hour, it's all over; this day will have cost us 37 out of the 40 tanks which were escorting the division.

As soon as our tanks are no more, our attention turns to the sky, a swarm of German planes are attacking ours, about ten in number. It's a massacre. The guns chatter; our planes are outnumbered ten to one! Five of ours are shot down immediately. We forget everything happening up front. With a lump in our throats, we watch these planes come crashing down in flames to the ground.

Everyone is dismayed, the battle is so unequal that we feel like asking for pardon for our planes, we would like to shout out to them; no, enough is enough, go home, don't try any more. We, the infantry, will stay here, you can't do anything, there are too few of you, go away.

Finally we at last examine our own position; we have piled into a dugout where there are men from the 49th, from the 39th, and the 18th Infantry Regiments. They, too, do not know where they are, what they are going to do, nor what they have in front of them.

They came here by night to attack in the morning, they awaited their orders, and are still waiting for them. While waiting, they saw us crossing the open plain, just as if we were at manoeuvres; they witnessed the carnage of our troops and confirm the madness of it all.

But suddenly their officers, seeing me arrive with some men, run up to me. They have a typical southern French accent. 'The Boches are hammering us, we have no ammunition, we're off, you are here, stay.'

Ah, but have I to take orders from them? I send them politely back to their positions with a warning that if their men run away I shall have them shot.

Speechless, they rejoin their posts, but before long, there's a great commotion and a general free-for all, with everyone running for his life. The officers shout to their men to come back, saying as they run past us that they too have no ammunition and are going. I can't help shouting back, 'You southern cowards'. But in front of us, a black wave is surging: the Boches are attacking. Two or three companies are advancing with bayonets fixed. I have no-one on my left. We are going to be outflanked and overrun.

'Get your machine-guns going, automatic rifles, fire here all of you, in the name of God, fire! fire! fire!' Everyone has understood and with the men that I have been able to regroup standing on the parapet, we fire away madly. Our rifles burn our hands, but we keep on firing, peppering the Boches with bullets. We see them being knocked down and fleeing back to their line in disorder. During all this time Pierre has not stopped shouting to me, 'Captain, don't let me be taken, I don't want to be a prisoner!'

Gosh! That was a close shave. We must reorganize ourselves. Will we have one moment's peace? Some troops join me and I organize the line. I have Pierre taken to a first-aid post. Alas, he was carrying my food and drink. I haven't got a thing and I am dreadfully thirsty. But I've a good bunch of men around me; men who if you set them an example, would do anything for you. They give me a drink (water is very precious) biscuits and some chocolate. I won't die of hunger.

Time marches on. Midday. One o'clock. The sun burns like fire. The artillery has concentrated its fire on Courcelles which is in flames. At 2 the steeple collapses, the village and the surrounding area are devastated.

What are we doing here? What are our orders? The Colonel? Everyone is seeking the Colonel. I have contacted the 6th and 10th Battalions, halted in front of Courcelles. My companies are in place. The 6th Battalion is looking for the Colonel. The 10th Battalion is looking for the Colonel, but he is nowhere to be found. We will shortly learn that on seeing the barrages, he took cover behind the railway-line at Tricot; he will only come and join me later at 2 p.m.

We get organized as best we can while awaiting our orders. The Boches are turning on the pressure and we are fighting them back with grenades. My God, what a day!

Soon we learn some sad news, brought by our communications messengers, it makes me very depressed; all the old 'uns of the regiment are no more. Two hours ago, I was shaking them by the hand, now they are nothing more than hunks of flesh, carcasses which will probably rot in the sun. All this in an hour, it's brutal, terrifying.

The hours pass slowly by; the Colonel, found at last, sheltering in a dug-out that the sappers have hastily built for him, sends us his orders.

We will attack again at 8 p.m. How and where, nobody knows!

Nothing is ready, everyone is seeking his orders—it's one awful confusion. The officers are looking for their men, the men for their officers. Everyone has different orders, and no one knows what precisely he has to do. There are no more N.C.O.s, the companies are reduced to 40 or 50 men.

Towards evening a new order: the attack is put off until tomorrow.

The front-line battalions return to our positions to spend the night.

Fresh rations? No question of it. How could the kitchens come out to us! We content ourselves by stocking up with grenades, cartridges, and weapons taken from the dead. When evening falls we stay put, overwhelmed by this day and haunted by the frightful vision of the slaughter which is due to start again tomorrow.

12 June

We are in very low spirits all night. This region which, a few days ago had not seen any fighting, suddenly found itself as a result of the German advance, in the front line. The only possible shelter would be in the village, but the deluge of gunfire is incessant and it would be madness to go there. Furthermore, there are regiments of all sorts, how would one find enough room for everyone?

Our regiment is sheltering in a trench 80 centimetres deep which can scarcely contain a battalion. Pushing and shoving the men crawl along on all fours so as not to expose themselves to the enemy's machine-guns. They try and find their wounded comrades who can't move on their own. How much devotion is shown during this night despite the enemy's furious gunfire. Ah, if they were to discover our position what butchery there would be.

With our minds fixed on yesterday's losses, our bodies aching, our limbs stiff, everyone is there, crouching, folded in two, waiting for the morrow, waiting for orders which can only be bad.

The hours pass, day will soon be dawning, no orders. It's only at 3 a.m. that these two terse lines are handed to each major: 'Proceed with your battalion as far as the front line to re-launch the attack.' That's all. Departure time, our positions and objectives, nothing. And daylight is with us, we haven't the time to consult one another, to transmit our orders. It's chaos again. Everyone moves forward haphazardly as best he can. We fall into shallowly dug trenches occupied by other troops in the sector. These immediately take fright, 'Take cover, you silly beggars, you'll get us spotted!' After a lot of jostling, we see that there just isn't enough room for everyone. The men go off in groups on their own to find some shelter, they are no longer under their chief's complete control.

4 a.m. It appears that the attack was due at this time. No one knew anything about it. However on the right some of our troops do attack and immediately Boche machine-guns spring into action. The alarm is given and their artillery pounds us, it seems as if we will all be wiped out. Our artillery doesn't fire a shell. The Boches are masters of the situation.

The attack is postponed; what could they expect from our division, decimated and without leaders? We stay put. We try and dig ourselves a hole and wait. The whole day planes are above us, and the artillery fire is relentless on Courcelles, a hurricane of fire passing over our heads.

I am at the northern edge of the village, the road is littered with bodies. It's unbelievable. There's a blown-up tank which is lying across and blocking the road. Inside are two burnt corpses, black, unrecognizable. Further on, bunches of men, legs twisted and mangled, or with gaping holes in their bodies, their eyeballs dangling out of their sockets, half their jaws missing, with terror written all over them; we can't take them away, they are too numerous, stretcher-bearers are sorely needed and the Boches don't give us a minute's peace. All we can do is to cover them with lime and then with a sheet or a blanket. We pick them up in mounds; but there are still more and more of them. Soon, under the burning sun, the flies will have a feast and the whole road will be nothing more than a cemetery of putrefying dead.

Further on, I fall into a pool of coagulated blood, it stinks. There's a dug-out beside it which has served as a first-aid post. The bodies are piled there in heaps, it's awful—we are forced to move on.

The few dug-outs which we do come across are already occupied by corpses from the previous day. You either have to squeeze in close to them or move on—but with each one we come to, it's the same thing.

Pierre is no longer with me. I go around alone or with a liaison officer, inspecting my battalion and regrouping the hesitant.

All day there are attacks on our right and left. We don't know a thing, there is shooting and grenades going off everywhere—we are living completely in the dark about everything, waiting, always waiting.

In the evening about 8 p.m. the regiment, the 6th and 10th Battalions, relieve the front line troops. My battalion, in reserve, is at the

Colonel's disposal, but he has found shelter in a cellar and doesn't come out any more.

But he continually sends for me to know if everything is going well, if everyone is in position and ready for anything. He is underground, as he isn't used to being so close to the enemy. Each time he sends for me—my post is 200 metres from his—I have to cross streets strewn with bodies and rubble, under heavy gunfire at the mercy of the first shell splinter. But what do others matter to him! He is in command and I have to obey.

13 June

All night an avalanche of shells fall on Courcelles, the houses are still in flames. This morning, we attacked with three divisions on our right near Méry. We don't know the result yet. We fear an attack on our flank at any moment.

The regiment has no more N.C.O.s, our losses are enormous, and eighteen days ago we left Mount Kemmel with a loss of 800 men.

At 7 p.m. the 18th Infantry Regiment attacks on our left to the north-east of Courcelles. It brings back 50 prisoners, but the Boches counter-attack and capture one of our lines. They are stuck in between our battalions and we have to force them out with grenades. This is the situation when night falls, a night of gunfire, of grenades exploding and of the thundering of guns.

I am now installed in a cellar with my liaison officer and my telephonists. The house above us has collapsed; the floor and the rubble are our only protection.

Inside, some old straw, mouldy and dirty. We have only been here twenty-four hours and we're already being eaten by the lice. Sleep is impossible with these continual alerts and heavy artillery fire. A single staircase descends into this dark hole; if it's blocked, we shall be choked to death. There's no time to be lost. Everyone takes a shovel or a pick and starts demolishing and digging. We shall only be happy when we have made a second way out.

14 June

We are expecting to be relieved. After an attack like ours one is usually relieved within forty-eight hours. The regiment needs to be reformed, we can't stay here. We await news of our departure, that's our main preoccupation at the moment.

15 June

Our hope of relief fades away. The division is positioned along a front 4 kilometres long from Courcelles to Méry. All the troops who were behind us have gone elsewhere. There is talk of German attacks on Amiens and Mount Kemmel.

We remain where we are harassed, exhausted and covered in vermin; thinking we would be here only forty-eight hours, we left everything behind. I haven't a thing, my trousers are torn and I have lost my greatcoat.

We scarcely see any newspapers here, but those we do see are enough. The journalists claim to have seen it all, but write idiotic articles on the wonderful advance of our troops, the last words of a dying soldier . . . let them come and live a short while with us, then we'll see.

We now know our losses on the 11th: as for the regiment, 19 officers (11 killed and 2 have since died); about 700 men out of action. In the division: 54 officers and more than 2,000 men. In the 121st Light Infantry Battalion, there is only one officer left—a sub-lieutenant who is commanding the battalion!

16 June

It's panic stations today. Enemy troop movements have been seen in front of us, near Rollot. Their planes are active, an attack is feared; orders come pouring in: an attack is certain, make ready.

Everyone is on edge; the Colonel sends for me yet again to organize the defence of the village—not really its defence but that of a single man—him, the Colonel! He is the only one that counts. I have to leave what I'm doing, the protection of the companies, exterior defences, and machine-gun emplacements. He is there in his cellar. If there's an attack, he must be protected. Orders to surround him with barbed wire, orders to build a redoubt in front of him with machine-guns in position; orders to have an escape trench built for him, with protecting fire on both sides of it.

He won't come out to see what's happening, but he repeatedly calls me in to see if everything is all right and that he will be well protected.

The men grumble; do they count? What disgust they feel in working for this man who doesn't care about them, who couldn't care less if they have only shallow holes for shelter with no protection.

It's war. Every man thinks of his own skin according to his means.

Fortunately it's calmer for the moment, the Boches are firing less. It has now been confirmed that our offensive caused a huge German attack to fail and stemmed their advance. We are now being smothered with praise to make us forget the madness of this attack.

18 June

The major returns from leave. I hand back the command of the battalion to him. He has missed the whole business. He tells us that the newspapers are full of the Mangin attacks, of these days which saved the situation. Alas! Who can suspect what we did, in what conditions we attacked. The regiment is reorganized in depth. We are placed in reserve in open fields on the Méry–Tricot road.

23 June

In the evening, we relieve the 121st Corps on Hill 100 (south-east of Courcelles).

Thus we are back in the lines, without a day of rest. The decimated battalion has been patched up as best it can. We don't know the N.C.O.s and they don't know the men.

At 10 p.m. I leave to inspect the lines. You have to go through the village to get to them; the lines themselves are in open fields, no dugouts, no protection.

Scattered everywhere across the plain are blown-up tanks, a mass of twisted metal. We count thirty of them in the sector.

26 June

Accompanied by one of my men, I set out at 9 p.m. to reconnoitre the lines. But we get lost, the night is very dark, and we can't see a thing. We have strayed from our line, made up of small posts 300 or 400 metres apart, and we can't find our way.

Not a sound, not a flare, nothing but corn all around us. Do we go forward, back, to the left or to the right? We are utterly lost. We don't dare move forwards for fear of meeting the Boche. My only weapons are my stick and my revolver; my companion has his rifle, but no cartridges. It's almost midnight. Are we going to spend the night like this and how shall we get back to our post in daylight? If we make any noise, our sentries may fire at us.

Suddenly, 100 metres from us, we hear shouts in German, three flares, some grenades exploding, a few rifle-shots, then silence falls again. Are we going to get it, have they seen us? However, thanks to the light from the flares, we recognize our positions, we are saved. We make for the post which had come under attack; the Boches had ambushed them amid the corn and surprised them at work. One dead corporal and another wounded soldier were brought back, but Dufour was captured by the Boches. Our men in the lines are jumpy as they have no protection.

21–22–23 July
At 9 p.m. we take up our positions in the second line at the lime-kilns.

We are now invaded by visitors. The sector is calm, the second line is attractive; these gents will be able to write a fine report on their return. Like snails after a storm, the gold braid is appearing from everywhere. They come by day and even at night, two, three every day. No shells, they are so happy to make themselves noticed . . . in the lines!

They go round gathering information: Ah! so that's your machine-gun there? Well I never . . . that's your 37 gun there, is it? And if you were to move it away a little? How many platoons have you in the lines? And where are the combat troops? And this and that . . . With all their information in their note-books, they scurry off back to their offices to announce that they have been to the lines and to write fine reports, stating the necessity of moving such a platoon, or modifying the position of a machine-gun.

Then we will receive orders, and counter-orders and no-one— except us—will know what really happens in the lines. It's a farce, an absolute farce.

2 August
Four years of war!!!

An attack is being prepared. The 5th Battalion is to carry it out. Have they gone off their heads? We must be dreaming. The chiefs have decided that the attack will be effected in total silence. How is it possible to make a battalion of men advance in silence without arousing the attention of the enemy?

Our objective is a small rectangular-shaped wood, about 1,200 metres from our lines. Without artillery preparation, the battalion must surround it and . . . bring back the goods. It's so simple—the German barrage, their machine-guns, nothing matters; just listen to the Colonel explaining the movement to us: you advance up to the wood, one company to the left, one to the right, you surround it and bring back everything inside. There you are, nothing simpler. You might think we were playing with toy soldiers on a table. Yet we have been at war for four years!

4 August

It's at 3 a.m. that the operation is due to begin.

The night is frighteningly dark. You can't see a metre ahead and we have to hold each other by our coat-tails so as not to lose the person in front. The major is very on edge, it's his first attack; up to the Kemmel he was adjutant to the Colonel, at Mount Kemmel he stayed in his dug-out, on 11 June he was on leave.

At 1.30 a.m. we reach Hill 100. The troops must be in place at 2.40, ready to leave at 3. Here we are on the plain, and it seems darker still, you can't even make out who your neighbour is. At 2.30, the two leading companies arrive. What a din! Hey! 3rd Squad, 55th, this way. Where are you, Germache? Everyone is looking and calling for everyone else and the Boches are in front of us. Real command is impossible. We shall advance—but where to? We don't know, it will be hit or miss. There are no land-marks, nothing but the darkness of the night.

Suddenly at 2.50 when the noise is louder still, with everyone trying to find his place, there is a great commotion—the Boches are on to us. They are attacking. All we can make out is their shouts and cries: Hurrah! Hoch! How many are they? Where are they? Pitch black. The major is overcome, he is dumbfounded, and not helped by his warrant-officer who has never seen the front except from the bottom of a dug-out.

It's not the moment to lose your head. Trillat (commanding the 18th) is at my side. A flare, in the name of God! The white flame lights up the night, German helmets are only 20 metres from us. Fire along the line, fire, fire, for Christ's sake, fire! Guns bark everywhere. The men take cover and the tide is stemmed, we have about 20 good men here who know what to do and won't be frightened off. A flare, fire again—it's finished. Where's the major, I haven't any idea. Now's the time to capture some prisoners. One platoon to the left another to the right, and forwards. Rendezvous in fifteen minutes at this spot.

Meanwhile, the telephone is ringing; the Colonel at the other end, in his dug-out 10 metres below ground, is fuming because we are not advancing. I let the major deal with him, I prefer the line. 'You must advance,' he says, 'at any price. Have you taken any Boches or machine-guns? Flank round to the right, blind them with your flares. You can't see clearly? Liaison is impossible? Too bad, advance nevertheless.' How easy it is to fight a war from a map at the bottom of a hole!

Meanwhile the two platoons return: they encountered the enemy and they have 6 men missing and 4 wounded. On our left a dreadful din starts; the Boches are attacking too and send us red and green rockets and flares. Day is about to dawn, their barrage opens fire. With explosions everywhere we are enveloped in smoke and fire, there is no question of advancing, we fall to the ground, making ourselves as small as possible.

A quarter of an hour later, calm returns, day is breaking, there's no time to be lost. We must be off and quickly, otherwise it will be too late.

At Méry, the Colonel is waiting for us. What a reception. Poor major who doesn't dare answer him back. 'You didn't manoeuvre properly,' he shouts, 'you should have done this and this. You'll start again in forty-eight hours.'

The major tells him of the machine-guns, of the Boches who disorganized the line, of the impossibility of doing anything in a night so dark . . . The Colonel is furious . . . 'Machine-guns? How many dead and wounded have you?' There is the heart of the matter; you've got to have a long list. No dead, and only a few wounded, you haven't done anything. Get your men blown to smithereens, you are a hero, your honour is safe. And this will always be the case.

In pursuit of the enemy
10 August to 5 September
Rollot–Boulogne-la-Grasse, La Poste, Bois des Loges, Ecuvilly, Bois du Quesnoy, Frétoy, Muirancourt, Guiscard

10 August
The lime-kiln . . . Méry . . . positioned in the second line . . . the battalion is now slowly climbing the slopes of Hill 100. The men file along the communication trenches a platoon at a time, with no one saying a word. Everyone's deep in thought. Soon it will be time to attack—there's plenty to think about.

Soon the companies will be massed, then there will be great anxiety as the time approaches. With all eyes riveted on the hands of a watch, we shall wait for the signal. Next, it will be up over the top of the trench and the great unknown. Just the plain ahead of you, and death perhaps.

The Boches are jumpy, their artillery fire is heavy, and as if shrapnel is not enough for them, they shower us with gas-shells. Unable to breathe, we are forced to put on our masks: our throats are scorched and our eyes are smarting. Puffing and blowing, we keep moving, and with perspiration streaming down under the mask, we hurry to get into position. We can't, however, stand the mask any more, it's suffocating us and we have to take it off.

At 1 a.m. we are in position. The enemy guns are now firing behind us, however in front there's nothing but hundreds of puffs of white smoke; gas-shells. In the thick of this fog, the troops have to be positioned for the attack. The major seems washed out; he's not used to it yet. As his side, his eternal warrant-officer repeatedly advises him to take cover in a shell-hole until it's time to leave. No, no, not that above all. One must not make the mistake of seeking cover, you don't come out afterwards. And, anyway, in moments such as this, the men want to see their leader, they need to feel supported, to feel their leader's gaze upon them.

I leave him to his meditation, to make a quick trip round the troops, it's very necessary. The lieutenant commanding the 17th Company is drunk, he needed a swig of rum to give himself some courage, another succeeded the first, then another and now there he is, sprawled in the trench, incapable of command. His officers and his N.C.O.s don't know what to do. My orders and threats (you don't joke in situations like this) have no effect—I'll have to do his job.

Finally everything is ready, everyone is at his post, the major himself is in the front line. We inspect the terrain, trying to find the best route and then settle down to wait.

At 4 a.m. day breaks. We take out our watches. Twenty liaison officers are there with the telephone wire unwound ready, everyone awaiting the crucial moment.

4.18 a.m., artillery preparation. Next it's the barrage which is to precede us. Everyone is silent, the Boches seem to have stopped firing; are they getting their breath so as to give us a really warm welcome? Our hearts are pounding. I'm confident, however, I remember the Kemmel where it worked so well.

4.30 a.m., three minutes to go, it's 4.33 that we go over the top. The major seems helpless. He clings close to his warrant-officer who is still advising him to stay behind. I leave him, as, at a time like this, one should feel courage and not cowardice. And the Boches are not firing any more, what are we risking?

4.31, 32. I climb over the parapet. Bayonets fixed! Ready for attack!

4.33, forward. The shout is repeated along the line, each man looking to see if his leader is coming too. Ah! if there was no one to command, what a day it would be! The platoons come out, some men are hesitant, but they see me, I push them forward with my stick, every one is out now. Every one? No, the poor major is there in a corner of the trench with his warrant-officer. He will only leave it when I return to tell him that the companies have achieved their objective, that I have found a shelter for him, and that he must not stay where he is.

At 5.08 a.m. the trenches of Aisne and Picardie are reached without mishap. The Boches have gone, and the trenches are empty. They only left a couple of machine-guns manned by two soldiers who, after having shot off a few rounds, surrender.

We wait, our gunners lengthen their range, our planes fly over at 50 metres and signal that there's no one there.

At 6 a.m. we attack our final objective, the square wood. A few Boches are there but they don't even fire at us.

The major and his warrant-officer seem nailed to the spot, I don't even bother with them any more—things are working well, now's the time to push forward. Attack, if you take cover you're frightened to come out afterwards; if you stay out, you are less likely to be afraid.

I send out reconnaissance parties in all directions, the troops are advancing too. With Trillat (in charge of the 18th) we go as far as Rollot. The countryside is empty. I inform the major of this, who tells me to come back! that we mustn't go so quickly.

7 a.m., 8 a.m., 9 a.m., the hours go by and we stay there without getting any orders. Come on, there are no more Germans, now's the time to advance. Are all the chiefs going to stay under cover and let the opportunity slip? What are they doing? How much time is being wasted?

11 a.m., midday, nothing. We are still waiting. I inform the Colonel of the situation.

It's only at 2 p.m. that we receive the order to advance. Is this the way to harass the Boches? If we had stuck close on their heels, how far might we have got?

The battalion has now formed into a column ready to march. I am with the advance guard. The Boches have withdrawn their artillery, it's not firing any more.

Rollot, Hainvilliers, Boulogne-la-Grasse. The cavalry comes into action; scouts are sent up ahead. The heat is overpowering. The men have to carry all their equipment, their rifles and machine-guns, they are whacked.

At Boulogne-la-Grasse, four armoured cars are put at my disposal. They scour the road and signal the enemy at Tilloloy wood.

We now advance with care; one company of marksmen has been formed. At La Poste we encounter some resistance from the enemy sentries who are falling back, and shortly afterwards, we make contact with the enemy who is occupying the fringe of Tilloloy wood.

It's almost 7 p.m. We have advanced 10 kilometres. We come under heavy fire from the Boches whose machine-guns open up as soon as they see us. We await orders.

It's 8, we form advance-posts at La Poste and organize our line. The enemy artillery starts shooting.

The terrain is dangerous; before leaving the Boches had mined all their dug-outs; a step hides a grenade, and the opening of a door sets off a bomb. They have thought of all the spots where we might go. We decide to dig ourselves a hole in the open, it's safer.

It's the beginning of a war of mobility. On our left, Montdidier is captured and overrun; to our right, the advance continues.

11 August

We bivouac on the spot. Orders and counter-orders flood in. Our positions are heavily bombarded.

10.45 a.m., sad news: Trillat, 'old man Trillat', has been killed. He and I were the only captains still alive after the battle of Mount Kemmel. Will it be my turn next? Poor old Trillat: in every attack he led his men fearlessly onwards, we saw him at the Chemin des Dames not even ducking when the machine-guns opened fire, at the Kemmel, urging his company on. And now, a shell has fallen right on him as he was having a bite to eat by the roadside! One of his officers has had an arm blown off.

All his men are shocked and have tears in their eyes at such a senseless end to a life. There he is, stretched out at our feet, with a gaping hole in his neck and half of his head missing. One can scarcely recognize him; what remains of his face is covered with blood, and blackened by powder.

11 a.m., we await our orders. The Boche is putting the pressure on, he is firing gas-shells at us, and seems determined to stay put.

There's not a senior officer in sight, we are on our own in the open countryside, and have no idea what is going on. Have they already found a nice dug-out somewhere?

The armoured cars go to reconnoitre ahead but no sooner have they crossed the Tilloloy wood, when they come under fire from guns, loaded with special bullets and they are forced to make a hasty retreat. One of them does not return. Hell for leather they rush back towards us, with shouts coming from inside: help, get some stretcher-bearers quickly. The driver and the other occupants are all severely wounded. The anti-tank bullets have pierced the armour-plating and ripped their limbs to pieces. We have great difficulty in getting them out of their little fort. One man has just died, his brains have been shot out, another is holding his leg in both hands. There's only his trousers stopping it from falling off.

There is blood everywhere; gaping holes in chests and stomachs, legs blown off, moaning and groaning: these men are suffering atrociously. They don't say much however, merely glancing from side to side in the hope of help, still hoping, hoping until the last!!

4.30 p.m. The 169th Infantry Division attacks in front of us and to the left. Tilloloy wood is an inferno, what can be happening in there?

The attack has failed, we try again at 8.30, but the result is the same. The Boches are digging their heels in, their artillery fire is very heavy.

14 August

I take command of the 10th Battalion, replacing Major Brébion who has been killed.

I have been recommended for the 'Légion d'Honneur' for the attack of 10 August. I will learn later on at Divisional H.Q. that you can receive this decoration only if you have lost a limb! That's how they recognize your devotion. If you haven't got an arm or leg missing, nothing doing.

18 August

The night is spent under a hail of shells; you would think that the Boches don't want to leave a tree standing.

At 6 p.m. an order arrives for us to attack tomorrow morning. The 10th Battalion must capture Buvier wood.

God! it's not going to be easy; a wide-open plain stretches before us and at about 1–1·5 kilometres in front, we can just make out the wood. What does it hide? How many machine-guns are hidden in its fringe? Doesn't my battalion risk being decimated as it advances? On our right we are in touch with the 297th; to our left, nothing, we form the pivot. In the centre of the plain, there's a small hillock, covered with bushes which promises nothing good. So, it's back to the unknown, to the race of death.

19 August
6.28! Attack!

The first wave surges forward. Scarcely have the men gone 100 metres when machine-gunfire sweeps the plain. Bullets whistle everywhere. The men are pinned down. On the hillock, each bush spits fire, the bullets virtually forming a net above our heads.

We manage to advance nevertheless. The German barrage opens up and we are enveloped in smoke. There are clods of earth flying everywhere, trees are shattered, bodies are thrown into the air, torn to ribbons—it's carnage.

Forward, forward! We've got to get out of this zone, otherwise not one of us will come back alive. Our troops are advancing admirably, crawling along on their stomachs, sowing death and injuries as they go! We are still making progress, but alas! so slowly. We are hardly 300 metres from our wood and Buvier wood is far away.

The company on our right presses on, it reaches the edge of the wood, when, unfortunately, its captain is killed by a machine-gun bullet; without someone to lead them, the platoons dive for cover and stay there.

It's 7 a.m., we can neither advance nor pull back. On all sides there are wounded dragging themselves back towards the rear. The Boches harass these crawling figures. They, too, must retain their position at all costs, even if they have to die doing it.

I send a messenger to the Colonel to advise him of our position. At midday, he sends me word that the 5th Battalion is going to attack on the right to help us. At the same time we are to join up with him and attack. How can I warn the companies?

Soon the 5th Battalion moves forward, but the German barrage opens up angrily. Gas! That's all we needed. We can't put our masks on as we would suffocate, it is so hot.

Is this all? Far from it! Enemy planes now come and fly low over us and empty their machine-guns on anything moving on the plain. Impossible to fire back, any movement we make is greeted by a hail of machine-gunfire. What a sticky situation to be in! Are we going to die here, flat on the ground, without being able to defend ourselves?

Day draws to its close, we have to get back to the lines, regroup and count our losses.

There are wounded, coming from everywhere. Their undressed wounds are hideous, they smell like corpses already.

The regiment can now display its list of victims! In my battalion alone there are 27 dead, 88 wounded, and 62 missing!

21 August
Towards 6 p.m. we learnt at last that the Boches are pulling back; the 5th and 6th Battalions now occupy Buvier wood. Major Brébion's replacement arrives this evening, I receive the order to rejoin the 5th Battalion and to boost Major Constantin's morale, who, according to the Colonel, is too depressed to command. Alas! Aren't we all at the same point?

22 August
I take up my post in the 5th Battalion; we are installed in a former Boche dug-out, swarming with bugs and fleas. It's so filthy that, in spite of the gunfire, we move to a shell crater.

We seem to have lost any notion of life. We are all so utterly exhausted, after days without rest and nights without sleep, that we haven't the strength to react.

This is our life: we are living in the open air, soaked by rain, and sweat. If no-one catches bronchitis or pneumonia, it will be a miracle!

23 August
Are we going to be relieved? Will someone at last admit that we are totally exhausted? Not at all, Major Constantin is sent back in disgrace, because he is too old and has been judged incapable of leading his men in an attack! I take command of the battalion.

24–25–26 August
Reinforcements arrive! Our losses since May are the following; Kemmel: 12 officers, 800 men. 11 June: 19 officers, 700 men. 10–25 August: 23 officers, 600–700 men. So, in less than four months: 54 officers and 2,200 men. The total strength of the regiment.

28 August

Great news: the Boches have taken to their heels.

At 6 a.m. we set off. The terrain is utterly devastated. Gas-shells, we advance with difficulty. Nevertheless, we cross Buvier wood, Ancy, Anvricourt. It's midday, the heat is overwhelming. Shells start falling and our advance becomes even more laborious. By evening we are at Ecuvilly. The 10th Battalion forms the advance guard, contact is made with the enemy and the advance is halted. It's only at 11 p.m. that we receive the order to make camp. We are in a little village, alone except for a few apple trees. I camp at the foot of one with my lieutenant machine-gunner and the Doc. Three holes have been dug for us which rather resemble a grave. It's raining and the water flows into these holes, we have to sleep in mud.

At 2 a.m. a note arrives. Under a blanket, with my torch pointing towards the bottom of my helmet, I read what it says: Attack for 5.30 a.m.! How can one give orders in such conditions! It's pitch black and impossible to write. . . .

We set off. But as soon as we leave Ecuvilly, we come under a hail of machine-gun and shell-fire. Men fall, but we press on. The wood is a few hundred metres away, and we must reach it. At last we are there; we pause to get our breath back then I decide to reconnoitre the wood so as I can position my companies, my officers accompany me. As we advance on the western fringe, there is a sudden volley of rifle-fire and one of my officers falls dead with a bullet through his heart. The Boches are in the wood, we have fallen into the trap. Furious, I report our situation to the Colonel. He simply replies, 'Since there are Boches there, take them prisoner and capture the wood!'

This would be laughable, if the situation weren't so tragic; night has fallen, we are exhausted and showered with shells and machine-gun bullets which are flying in all directions, the men have had enough. Attack? To venture an advance through this wood in the dead of night? It would be madness. Let us wait for daylight.

30 August

Our attacks on the right and left are maintained, but without success; the Germans are dug-in at the north canal and are holding it steadfastly. What are our attacks worth? Our exhaustion is total and we can only succeed when the enemy gives way under our artillery fire.

At 6 p.m. the enemy unleash an avalanche of fire on the wood, there is gas swirling everywhere: coughing, spitting, and vomiting with our insides seemingly on fire, our fatigue gets the better of us. Our losses are great and many are seriously wounded. Everyone is bitter at seeing his comrades fall one after the other. Will this be the fate of us all?

I have no more N.C.O.s, with my platoons reduced to half a squad, everything is becoming impossible. No-one wants to leave his emplacement any more and it's only by threats that I can make myself obeyed, and it's hard to do this when you share their state of exhaustion.

My situation is the following: I have only two officers left! a lieutenant commanding the machine-gunners and a captain, who arrived two days ago, commanding the 18th Company.

My last captain had his arm blown off and lost a leg. My two other companies are commanded one by a warrant-officer who is hastily sent to me from the 16th, the other by a sergeant.

As for N.C.O.s, one sergeant per company plus two corporals. As far as troops are concerned: 25 men in two companies, 30–35 in the other two! That's all that remains of the battalion after the reinforcements we received six days ago! How can one carry out orders in such conditions, how can one attack? The battalion has scarcely the effective strength of one company.

31 August

The men can't take any more: there have been cases of men breaking down in tears and rolling on the ground sobbing. As a result of seeing their comrades killed and maimed, their nerves have been broken. We have hordes of wounded, but we have to go 2 kilometres to the rear in order to get medical attention. There was one good fellow in the regiment, Doctor Maupin, but he was killed on 11 June; those who have been sent since prefer the shelter of a cellar. I sent an order for one of them to come here and work; he came only to leave again, on the pretext that he needed water and more dressings. And in the meanwhile the men are in agony, but there is no-one to ease their suffering.

At 7 a.m. we attack again. Our infantry gains ground towards Campagne on our right. We ourselves capture the last machine-guns which were standing between us and the path bordering the canal.

4 September

At 6.15 I receive the order to advance. With my skeleton battalion, we occupy the mill at the north canal, then the lock. The pursuit is on again, the Boches have gone. By 10 a.m. we have crossed Frétoy, then Réjavoine. At midday we are at Muirancourt where the enemy welcomes us with a few shells. Finally at 6 p.m., we have gone beyond Guiscard. My battalion holds Chateau-Mesuy, Hill 104, Bethancourt.

Our advance has been 8 kilometres, we are as tired as if we had done a forced march of 50.

At nightfall, the 297th passes in front of us, we stay where we are. Some Boche dug-outs permit us to get some sleep; we are no longer in the front line, we can breathe.

The following order arrives at 11 p.m.: tomorrow the division will regroup. What does this mean? Aren't we going to get some rest even now? Our weariness is indescribable. Our advance from Courcelles has been about 30–35 kilometres.

5 September

We bivouac on the spot, awaiting orders and receiving supplies.

At last at 4 p.m., we receive the order to leave. What joy! We are going to the rear. Everyone's running around, bursting to tell the good news.

It's not the moment to cop it; some shells explode, men and mules fall to the ground.

Let's get out of here. The artillery fire does not stop, what does it matter, we are going to the rear. We find the strength to walk again. Shortly afterwards we are out of the firing zone, we can breathe. What a relief to feel oneself away from it all. Jokes are cracked; we pass our men and artillery, the plain is in front of us. How good it feels, let's get as far away as possible!

Lorraine Sector

7 September to 16 November

14 September

Is this a sector at all? In broad daylight we can walk along the roads under the very noses of the Boches without a shot being fired. We are lodged in huts and nobody thinks of using the dug-outs; the kitchens are installed right in the front line. Their chimneys belch smoke, but nobody bothers. Over the way, the Boches do the same, it's a rest sector. You would think you are on stage at the theatre! There's not a shell-hole to be seen in the trenches or along the paths. It's just the sort of sector for the President of the Republic or for parliamentary missions.

On 16 September, I get sixteen days leave (six days for being mentioned in dispatches at Mount Kemmel, 11 June, and the pursuit).

6 October
I rejoin the regiment at Drouville, in the Serres sector. The 359th Infantry Regiment ceased its existence on the 4th! It has been disbanded and replaced by the 14th Tirailleurs who are on their way here from Oran. We don't know if we shall be amalgamated with them or be sent to another regiment.

7–8–9 October
My relationship with the new major who has been appointed to lead us is becoming more and more strained. We are not speaking to each other any more. I have requested to change battalions, and am awaiting an answer.

The Colonel informs me that he has again proposed me for the 'Légion d'Honneur' but his recommendation didn't get further than the first desk at Divisional H.Q. Only those who have lost a limb or some faculty have the right to be granted it.

The days pass uneventfully by. I spend my mornings hunting. The plains are full of partridge, you can even hunt between the lines, the Boches don't mind! they do it too! Every morning I bring back a hare and three or four partridges. Everyone hunts in this area, especially those from the rear. The police are on the alert and hunt the hunters. But here there's nothing to fear, they won't come as far as this.

15 October
I am informed by the Colonel that my request has been granted. I leave the major and his battalion. He tells me too that I have been proposed to take command of my own battalion.

With my name already on the list, I can be chosen any day now. In the meanwhile, the General wants to send me to Divisional H.Q. to reorganize the instruction centre there and to deliver lectures.

Is this the beginning of the end for me? No, for it is clear that I won't even set foot inside Divisional H.Q., as the Colonel declares he doesn't want to lose me and is going to request my transfer to the 14th Tirailleurs, the 1st Battalion of which has been formed.

21 October
Colonel Dineaux summons me to replace Major Rouchon who is leaving the regiment. My function is that of the Colonel's chief assistant officer.

22–23–24 October
Office life. Shut in all day, surrounded by papers, examining maps, compiling dossiers. Now it's my turn to send for reports and notes! My turn to prepare attacks and order reconnaissances.

An attack is planned for November, our future advance has to be worked out. Ludendorff is overrun. Our hopes increase that the end is nigh, but in the meanwhile there is fighting all along the front and it's moving towards us.

We are due to attack along the whole Lorraine Front with two armies and the Americans, 600,000 men, with as many again in reserve, so they say.

The artillery is massing, all calibres are arriving. There are gunners, guns, and piles of shells everywhere. Every night lorries pour in with thousands of projectiles. By day our planes keep watch.

The most extraordinary thing about it is that all this is happening so peacefully. The Boches are letting us carry out all these preparations without firing a shot.

1–2–3 November
General Mangin is reported as being in the vicinity. Soon we'll be forced to leave the quiet life to set out again for the unknown, and to relive the misery of an attack.

In front of us we can distinguish the silhouettes of the Lorraine forests; how many machine-guns are hidden in there?

The attack is set for the 6th, then postponed until the 8th, then the 10th.

Then we suddenly learn that Germany is sending envoys to discuss an armistice. Foch has given them seventy-two hours to sign. This is the only thing in our minds at present. If the armistice is signed, it's peace; if not, it's an immediate attack, and butchery in all its horror.

10 November
There's been a real firework display going on over in the German lines all night long. They are letting off all their flares and rockets, green, red, yellow, they all mingle in the sky. A few Boches try to

come and fraternizè with our troops, but they are chased off by rifle fire.

Then we learn that Revolution is brewing in Germany, that the Emperor is abdicating. It's over, the Boches are withdrawing everywhere.

We are excited, we wait and hope.

11 November

Firework display continued all night over in the enemy camp. At 6 a.m., we hear on the radio that the armistice has been signed. The end of hostilities is fixed for 11 a.m.

At 11 a.m. it's all over, we are no longer at war. What joy—the champagne flows, the attack won't take place. There's a smile on everyone's lips, no more fighting, we'll be able to move without fearing a bullet, a shell, a rocket, or gas—the war is over!

The Boches have thirty days to sign the peace treaty.

13–14–15 November

Alas, we are not there yet. I rejoin the 2nd Battalion of Tirailleurs.

My battalion commanding officer, Gérard, is a charming fellow. But it's back to the pettiness of peacetime: parades, exercises, spit and polish, etc. We camp at Serres. Nothing to do the whole day, no guarding of the sector. Every day we hope that it will be our turn to leave. We play endless games of poker—it's the only thing one can do.

At last, on 16 November, we receive the order to be ready to leave on the following day.

Occupation
17 November 1918 to 23 January 1919

17 November

We leave Serres at 6 a.m. We cross Arraucourt, then the German lines. We can't believe our eyes when we see the extent of the barbed-wire entanglements and fortifications in this supposedly calm sector; they represent three years' work and we would have had to take them by force! How good it is to saunter through them with your cane in your hand.

As we proceed, a few curious onlookers appear. The Germans have taken everything with them. There's not a single gun or weapon of value remaining. Only the ammunition dumps which they couldn't destroy have been left.

We camp at Mulcey. The inhabitants welcome us with open arms, but they have been robbed of everything. They welcome us with words and they certainly have some stories to tell. Here, butter costs 18 marks a pound and shoes 200 marks a pair. It's very cold. This walk which should be pleasant, is rather disagreeable.

18 November

We are going to be billeted at Guermange. All the towns are decked out in the French colours, and the inhabitants are on their doorsteps.

At Guermange, the whole village is in festive mood. We are received by the local dignitaries. Each one has got out his coat, top-hat, and his Sunday-best suit. Everyone young and old, is wearing a rosette. The children, led by the village priest, are carrying little French flags.

Unbeknown to the Boches, the young girls of the village had made dresses in the French colours; when they learnt of the armistice they prepared a welcome for the first French troops.

As the major, quite overcome by the occasion, makes his speech, they surround him and each one has her compliment to pay and a bouquet of flowers to offer.

It's charming for a village of 300 inhabitants. What will it be like when we are surrounded by thousands? These folk, however, are simplicity itself and tell us all they have suffered and endured. Each one has his own sad tale to tell.

As we advance, so prices rise. If the French soldier is well received, people are starting to exploit him.

19–20–21 November

We stay at Guermange. It is said that they don't want us to have any contact with the Boches, so we are waiting until they leave.

We resume exercises, not very enthusiastically—it's merely to keep the men occupied. Our men? They are coloured troops from Africa who don't speak much French, who are lazy and light-fingered.

They say that from 1 December leave will be for twenty days.

1 December

We enter Bavaria. The Boches stare at us with curiosity. You can feel their pride. Here only German is spoken, and the men can't make themselves understood.

2 December
Billeted at Vogelbach. We are guarding the outposts. Not a word of French here. As we pass through the villages, some inhabitants cry, 'Long live France', but others turn their heads.

6 December
Our billets are at Rottweiler. Here the people are German at heart and one can feel their animosity.

The main point of discussion is money. The mark is worth 0·70 francs, but they don't want to understand and demand its nominal value, 1·25 francs. There are long arguments. An interpreter is sent for, but they get kid-glove treatment, no one daring to impose his will upon them. No trouble, no trouble. What would they do however, if they were occupying our country? Here, it's the Frenchman who is fleeced.

When you think of the way they have acted, of the suffering they inflicted on our compatriots, four years of insults, of fines, of ill-treatment of every sort, it makes you sick.

If we react strongly, the Germans complain, then it's a report to the Colonel, an inquest to be held in the Division, and the paperwork piles up on every desk.

And yet these people here don't know what war is; they haven't seen barbed wire or trenches, all the fields are cultivated. We are the victors, they won't even feel it and we yield before their demands.

7–8–9 December
Exercises again, leave is slow in coming through. The authorities declare: Not enough transport. To which the troops reply: When it was a question of sending us to Ba-li-bou you managed to find trains and vehicles then, but when it's our leave, you don't give a damn!

We stay at Otterberg. Captain Gérard and I are lodged with a factory-owner, who, fawning and contemptible, put everything at our disposal: bathroom, billiard-room. He offers us cigars, venison—the Boche in all his beauty. One feels that these sort of people will sign anything you ask of them, but won't do a thing about it. They have a strong sense of discipline, as we pass by, people salute us. If we complain that the village is dirty, a quarter of an hour later all the people are sweeping the streets and washing.

There are kids swarming everywhere, in the houses, on the streets.

On 10 December, we receive an order to proceed to Kaiserslautern to welcome General Fayolle. He is due to make his entry at 2 p.m. The streets are full of people, expecting something impressive. Time goes by, 2.30, 3, 4 o'clock, nothing. Finally in the evening, his arrival is announced, everyone cranes his neck, the troops present arms, a limousine arrives, flashes past, it's all over. It's a passing shadow, no-one was even able to distinguish that a French general was in the car. What a loss of prestige in the Boches' eyes!

1919

13 January
These days are my last, men are being sent home and my turn will come shortly. There are exercises every day, so we don't get out of the habit.

On 20 January I go and lunch with the Colonel, on the 21st with the General. It's over now. I haven't a friend left, my comrades from the 359th have disappeared, either killed or wounded or posted to other corps. I have no regrets about leaving this regiment where I don't know a soul.

The General has just informed me that he has again put my name forward for the 'Légion d'Honneur' and that this time I should get it. Nevertheless I am going home with my five mentions in dispatches, three years at the front, and still no red ribbon.

On 23 January I am paid, a few handshakes. The road is open for me to rejoin civilian life which I left some four and a half years ago.

23 January
I put myself at the disposal of the major in charge of transport to carry a detachment of troops home.

There are threats flying everywhere; the men going home speak only of Bolshevism, of revolution: 'We'll show the bosses! Our comrades won't have died in the trenches in vain.'

Hatred and threats are on many lips.

30 January
I am demobbed from the 163rd Infantry Regiment at Nice.

Formalities, paperwork, queues at desks of all sorts to get my final pay and gratuity booklet, to be returned to civilian life.

At last it's finished. I have fulfilled my duty. I am no longer a soldier.

11 February

13.411 D. 'Chevalier de la Légion d'Honneur'; 'Croix de Guerre avec Palme'; 'Outstanding officer, of proven courage. Frequently distinguished himself in the battles of which he was part, notably when in command of a battalion during the attack of 11 June 1918. Particularly distinguished himself at Verdun, on the Aisne, at Mount Kemmel, at Guiscard, at Montdidier. Mentioned five times in dispatches.'

Index

Army Divisions, etc, mentioned